On
Managing
Yourself
(Vol. 2)

HBR's 10 Must Reads series is the definitive collection of ideas and best practices for aspiring and experienced leaders alike. These books offer essential reading selected from the pages of *Harvard Business Review* on topics critical to the success of every manager.

Titles include:

HBR's 10 Must Reads 2015
HBR's 10 Must Reads 2016
HBR's 10 Must Reads 2017
HBR's 10 Must Reads 2018
HBR's 10 Must Reads 2019
HBR's 10 Must Reads 2020
HBR's 10 Must Reads 2021
HBR's 10 Must Reads for CEOs
HBR's 10 Must Reads for New Managers
HBR's 10 Must Reads on AI, Analytics, and the New Machine Age
HBR's 10 Must Reads on Boards
HBR's 10 Must Reads on Building a Great Culture
HBR's 10 Must Reads on Business Model Innovation
HBR's 10 Must Reads on Career Resilience
HBR's 10 Must Reads on Change Management (Volumes 1 and 2)
HBR's 10 Must Reads on Collaboration
HBR's 10 Must Reads on Communication (Volumes 1 and 2)
HBR's 10 Must Reads on Creativity
HBR's 10 Must Reads on Design Thinking
HBR's 10 Must Reads on Diversity
HBR's 10 Must Reads on Emotional Intelligence
HBR's 10 Must Reads on Entrepreneurship and Startups
HBR's 10 Must Reads on Innovation
HBR's 10 Must Reads on Leadership (Volumes 1 and 2)
HBR's 10 Must Reads on Leadership for Healthcare
HBR's 10 Must Reads on Leadership Lessons from Sports
HBR's 10 Must Reads on Lifelong Learning

HBR's 10 Must Reads on Making Smart Decisions
HBR's 10 Must Reads on Managing Across Cultures
HBR's 10 Must Reads on Managing in a Downturn, Expanded
  Edition
HBR's 10 Must Reads on Managing People (Volumes 1 and 2)
HBR's 10 Must Reads on Managing Risk
HBR's 10 Must Reads on Managing Yourself (Volumes 1 and 2)
HBR's 10 Must Reads on Mental Toughness
HBR's 10 Must Reads on Negotiation
HBR's 10 Must Reads on Nonprofits and the Social Sectors
HBR's 10 Must Reads on Organizational Resilience
HBR's 10 Must Reads on Platforms and Ecosystems
HBR's 10 Must Reads on Public Speaking and Presenting
HBR's 10 Must Reads on Reinventing HR
HBR's 10 Must Reads on Sales
HBR's 10 Must Reads on Strategic Marketing
HBR's 10 Must Reads on Strategy (Volumes 1 and 2)
HBR's 10 Must Reads on Strategy for Healthcare
HBR's 10 Must Reads on Teams
HBR's 10 Must Reads on Women and Leadership
HBR's 10 Must Reads: The Essentials

On
Managing
Yourself
(Vol. 2)

HARVARD BUSINESS REVIEW PRESS
Boston, Massachusetts

Copyright 2021 Harvard Business School Publishing Corporation
All rights reserved
Printed and bound in India by Replika Press Pvt. Ltd.
10 9 8 7 6 5 4 3

The web addresses referenced in this book were live and correct at the time of the book's publication but may be subject to change.

Cataloging-in-Publication data is forthcoming.

ISBN: 978-1-64782-080-0
eISBN: 978-1-64782-081-7

Contents

On
Managing
Yourself
(Vol. 2)

From Purpose to Impact

by Nick Craig and Scott Snook

The two most important days in your life are the day you are born and the day you find out why.

—Mark Twain

OVER THE PAST FIVE YEARS, there's been an explosion of interest in purpose-driven leadership. Academics argue persuasively that an executive's most important role is to be a steward of the organization's purpose. Business experts make the case that purpose is a key to exceptional performance, while psychologists describe it as the pathway to greater well-being.

Doctors have even found that people with purpose in their lives are less prone to disease. Purpose is increasingly being touted as the key to navigating the complex, volatile, ambiguous world we face today, where strategy is ever changing and few decisions are obviously right or wrong.

Despite this growing understanding, however, a big challenge remains. In our work training thousands of managers at organizations from GE to the Girl Scouts, and teaching an equal number of executives and students at Harvard Business School, we've found that fewer than 20% of leaders have a strong sense of their own individual purpose. Even fewer can distill their purpose into a concrete statement. They may be able to clearly articulate their organization's mission: Think of Google's "To organize the world's information

1

and make it universally accessible and useful," or Charles Schwab's "A relentless ally for the individual investor." But when asked to describe their own purpose, they typically fall back on something generic and nebulous: "Help others excel." "Ensure success." "Empower my people." Just as problematic, hardly any of them have a clear plan for translating purpose into action. As a result, they limit their aspirations and often fail to achieve their most ambitious professional and personal goals.

Our purpose is to change that—to help executives find and define their leadership purpose and put it to use. Building on the seminal work of our colleague Bill George, our programs initially covered a wide range of topics related to authentic leadership, but in recent years purpose has emerged as the cornerstone of our teaching and coaching. Executives tell us it is the key to accelerating their growth and deepening their impact, in both their professional and personal lives. Indeed, we believe that the process of articulating your purpose and finding the courage to live it—what we call *purpose to impact*—is the single most important developmental task you can undertake as a leader.

Consider Dolf van den Brink, the president and CEO of Heineken USA. Working with us, he identified a decidedly unique purpose statement—"To be the wuxia master who saves the kingdom"—which reflects his love of Chinese kung fu movies, the inspiration he takes from the wise, skillful warriors in them, and the realization that he, too, revels in high-risk situations that compel him to take action. With that impetus, he was able to create a plan for reviving a challenged legacy business during extremely difficult economic conditions. We've also watched a retail operations chief call on his newly clarified purpose—"Compelled to make things better, whomever, wherever, however"—to make the "hard, cage-rattling changes" needed to beat back a global competitor. And we've seen a factory director in Egypt use his purpose—"Create families that excel"—to persuade employees that they should honor the 2012 protest movement not by joining the marches but by maintaining their loyalties to one another and keeping their shared operation running.

We've seen similar results outside the corporate world. Kathi Snook (Scott's wife) is a retired army colonel who'd been struggling to reengage in work after several years as a stay-at-home mom. But

Idea in Brief

The Problem

Purpose is increasingly seen as the key to navigating the complex world we face today, where strategy is ever changing and few decisions are obviously right or wrong. At the same time, few leaders have a strong sense of their own leadership purpose or a clear plan for translating it into action. As a result, they often fail to achieve their most ambitious professional and personal goals.

The Solution

The first step toward uncovering your leadership purpose is to mine your life story for major themes

that reveal your lifelong passions and values. Next, craft a concise purpose statement that leaves you emboldened and energized. Finally, develop a *purpose-to-impact plan*. Effective plans:

- Use language that is uniquely meaningful to you

- Focus on big-picture aspirations and then set shorter-term goals, working backward with increasing specificity

- Emphasize the strengths you bring to the table

- Take a holistic view of work and family

after nailing her purpose statement—"To be the gentle, behind-the-scenes, kick-in-the-ass reason for success," something she'd done throughout her military career and with her kids—she decided to run for a hotly contested school committee seat, and won.

And we've implemented this thinking across organizations. Unilever is a company that is committed to purpose-driven leadership, and Jonathan Donner, the head of global learning there, has been a key partner in refining our approach. Working with his company and several other organizations, we've helped more than 1,000 leaders through the purpose-to-impact process and have begun to track and review their progress over the past two to three years. Many have seen dramatic results, ranging from two-step promotions to sustained improvement in business results. Most important, the vast majority tell us they've developed a new ability to thrive in even the most challenging times.

In this article, we share our step-by-step framework to start you down the same path. We'll explain how to identify your purpose and then develop an impact plan to achieve concrete results.

What Is Purpose?

Most of us go to our graves with our music still inside us, unplayed.
—Oliver Wendell Holmes

Your leadership purpose is who you are and what makes you distinctive. Whether you're an entrepreneur at a start-up or the CEO of a *Fortune* 500 company, a call center rep or a software developer, your purpose is your brand, what you're driven to achieve, the magic that makes you tick. It's not *what* you do, it's *how* you do your job and *why*—the strengths and passions you bring to the table no matter where you're seated. Although you may express your purpose in different ways in different contexts, it's what everyone close to you recognizes as uniquely you and would miss most if you were gone.

When Kathi shared her purpose statement with her family and friends, the response was instantaneous and overwhelming: "Yes! That's you—all business, all the time!" In every role and every context—as captain of the army gymnastics team, as a math teacher at West Point, informally with her family and friends—she had always led from behind, a gentle but forceful catalyst for others' success. Through this new lens, she was able to see herself—and her future—more clearly. When Dolf van den Brink revealed his newly articulated purpose to his wife, she easily recognized the "wuxia master" who had led his employees through the turmoil of serious fighting and unrest in the Congo and was now ready to attack the challenges at Heineken USA head-on.

At its core, your leadership purpose springs from your identity, the essence of who you are. Purpose is not a list of the education, experience, and skills you've gathered in your life. We'll use ourselves as examples: The fact that Scott is a retired army colonel with an MBA and a PhD is not his purpose. His purpose is "to help others live more 'meaning-full' lives." Purpose is also not a professional title, limited to your current job or organization. Nick's purpose is not "To lead the Authentic Leadership Institute." That's his job. His purpose is "To wake you up and have you find that you are home." He has been doing just that since he was a teenager, and if you sit next to him on the shuttle from Boston to New York, he'll wake you up (figuratively), too. He simply can't help himself.

Purpose is definitely not some jargon-filled catch-all ("Empower my team to achieve exceptional business results while delighting our customers"). It should be specific and personal, resonating with you and you alone. It doesn't have to be aspirational or cause-based ("Save the whales" or "Feed the hungry"). And it's not what you think it should be. It's who you can't help being. In fact, it might not necessarily be all that flattering ("Be the thorn in people's side that keeps them moving!").

How Do You Find It?

To be nobody but yourself in a world which is doing its best, night and day, to make you everybody else, means to fight the hardest battle which any human being can fight; and never stop fighting.

—E.E. Cummings

Finding your leadership purpose is not easy. If it were, we'd all know exactly why we're here and be living that purpose every minute of every day. As E.E. Cummings suggests, we are constantly bombarded by powerful messages (from parents, bosses, management gurus, advertisers, celebrities) about what we should be (smarter, stronger, richer) and about how to lead (empower others, lead from behind, be authentic, distribute power). To figure out who you are in such a world, let alone "be nobody but yourself," is indeed hard work. However, our experience shows that when you have a clear sense of who you are, everything else follows naturally.

Some people will come to the purpose-to-impact journey with a natural bent toward introspection and reflection. Others will find the experience uncomfortable and anxiety-provoking. A few will just roll their eyes. We've worked with leaders of all stripes and can attest that even the most skeptical discover personal and professional value in the experience. At one multinational corporation, we worked with a senior lawyer who characterized himself as "the least likely person to ever find this stuff useful." Yet he became such a supporter that he required all his people to do the program. "I have never read a self-help book, and I don't plan to," he told his staff. "But if you want to become an exceptional leader, you have to know your leadership purpose." The key to engaging both the dreamers and the skeptics is to build a process that has room to express individuality but also offers step-by-step practical guidance.

The first task is to mine your life story for common threads and major themes. The point is to identify your core, lifelong strengths, values, and passions—those pursuits that energize you and bring you joy. We use a variety of prompts but have found three to be most effective:

- What did you especially love doing when you were a child, before the world told you what you should or shouldn't like or do? Describe a moment and how it made you feel.

- Tell us about two of your most challenging life experiences. How have they shaped you?

- What do you enjoy doing in your life now that helps you sing your song?

We strongly recommend grappling with these questions in a small group of a few peers, because we've found that it's almost impossible for people to identify their leadership purpose by themselves. You can't get a clear picture of yourself without trusted colleagues or friends to act as mirrors.

After this reflective work, take a shot at crafting a clear, concise, and declarative statement of purpose: "My leadership purpose is ____." The words in your purpose statement must be yours. They must capture your essence. And they must call you to action.

To give you an idea of how the process works, consider the experiences of a few executives. When we asked one manager about her childhood passions, she told us about growing up in rural Scotland and delighting in "discovery" missions. One day, she and a friend set out determined to find frogs and spent the whole day going from pond to pond, turning over every stone. Just before dark, she discovered a single frog and was triumphant. The purpose statement she later crafted—"Always find the frogs!"—is perfect for her current role as the senior VP of R&D for her company.

Another executive used two "crucible" life experiences to craft her purpose. The first was personal: Years before, as a divorced young mother of two, she found herself homeless and begging on the street, but she used her wits to get back on her feet. The second was professional: During the economic crisis of 2008, she had to oversee her company's retrenchment from Asia and was tasked with closing the flagship operation in the region. Despite the near hopeless job environment, she was able to help every one of her employees find another job before letting them go. After discussing these stories with her group, she shifted her purpose statement from "Continually and consistently develop and facilitate the growth and development of myself and others leading to great performance" to "With tenacity, create brilliance."

Dolf came to his "wuxia master" statement after exploring not only his film preferences but also his extraordinary crucible experience in the Congo, when militants were threatening the brewery he managed and he had to order it barricaded to protect his employees and prevent looting. The Egyptian factory director focused on family as his purpose because his stories revealed that familial love and

Purpose statements

From bad . . .	To good
Lead new markets department to achieve exceptional business results	Eliminate "chaos"
Be a driver in the infrastructure business that allows each person to achieve their needed outcomes while also mastering the new drivers of our business as I balance my family and work demands	Bring water and power to the 2 billion people who do not have it
Continually and consistently develop and facilitate the growth and development of myself and others, leading to great performance	With tenacity, create brilliance

7

support had been the key to facing every challenge in his life, while the retail operations chief used "Compelled to improve" after realizing that his greatest achievements had always come when he pushed himself and others out of their comfort zones.

As you review your stories, you will see a unifying thread, just as these executives did. Pull it, and you'll uncover your purpose. (The exhibit "Purpose statements: from bad to good" offers sampling of purpose statements.)

How Do You Put Your Purpose into Action?

This is the true joy in life, the being used for a purpose recognized by yourself as a mighty one.

—George Bernard Shaw

Clarifying your purpose as a leader is critical, but writing the statement is not enough. You must also envision the impact you'll have on your world as a result of living your purpose. Your actions—not your words—are what really matter. Of course, it's virtually impossible for any of us to fully live into our purpose 100% of the time. But with work and careful planning, we can do it more often, more consciously, wholeheartedly, and effectively.

Purpose-to-impact plans differ from traditional development plans in several important ways: They start with a statement of leadership purpose rather than of a business or career goal. They take a holistic view of professional and personal life rather than ignore the fact that you have a family or outside interests and commitments. They incorporate meaningful, purpose-infused language to create a document that speaks to you, not just to any person in your job or role. They force you to envision long-term opportunities for living your purpose (three to five years out) and then help you to work backward from there (two years out, one year, six months, three months, 30 days) to set specific goals for achieving them.

When executives approach development in this purpose-driven way, their aspirations—for instance, Kathi's decision to get involved in the school board, or the Egyptian factory director's ambition to

Purpose-to-impact planning	Traditional development planning
Uses meaningful, purpose-infused language	Uses standard business language
Is focused on strengths to realize career aspirations	Is focused on weaknesses to address performance
Elicits a statement of leadership purpose that explains how you will lead	States a business- or career-driven goal
Sets incremental goals related to living your leadership purpose	Measures success using metrics tied to the firm's mission and goals
Focuses on the future, working backward	Focuses on the present, working forward
Is unique to you; addresses who you are as a leader	Is generic; addresses the job or role
Takes a holistic view of work and family	Ignores goals and responsibilities outside the office

run manufacturing and logistics across the Middle East—are stoked. Leaders also become more energized in their current roles. Dolf's impact plan inspired him to tackle his role at Heineken USA with four mottos for his team: "Be brave," "Decide and do," "Hunt as a pack," and "Take it personally." When Unilever executive Jostein Solheim created a development plan around his purpose—"To be part of a global movement that makes changing the world seem fun and achievable"—he realized he wanted to stay on as CEO of the Ben & Jerry's business rather than moving up the corporate ladder.

Let's now look at a hypothetical purpose-to-impact plan (representing a composite of several people with whom we've worked) for an in-depth view of the process. "Richard" arrived at his purpose only after being prodded into talking about his lifelong passion for sailing; suddenly, he'd found a set of experiences and language that could redefine how he saw his job in procurement.

Richard's development plan leads with the **purpose statement** he crafted: "To harness all the elements to win the race." This is followed by **an explanation** of why that's his purpose: Research shows

A Purpose-to-Impact Plan

THIS SAMPLE PLAN shows how "Richard" uses his unique leadership purpose to envision big-picture aspirations and then work backward to set more-specific goals.

1. Create purpose statement
To harness all the elements to win the race

2. Write explanation
I love to sail. In my teens and 20s, I raced high-performance three-man skiffs and almost made it to the Olympics. Now sailing is my hobby and passion—a challenge that requires discipline, balance, and coordination. You never know what the wind will do next, and in the end, you win the race only by relying on your team's combined capabilities, intuition, and flow. It's all about how you read the elements.

3. Set three- to five-year goals
Be known for training the best crews and winning the big races: Take on a global procurement role and use the opportunity to push my organization ahead of competitors

How will I do it?

- Make everyone feel they're part of the same team
- Navigate unpredictable conditions by seeing wind shears before everyone else
- Keep calm when we lose individual races; learn and prepare for the next ones

Celebrate my shore team: Make sure the family has one thing we do that binds us

4. Set two-year goals
Win the gold: Implement a new procurement model, redefining our relationship with suppliers and generating 10% cost savings for the company

Tackle next-level racing challenge: Move into a European role with broader responsibilities

How will I do it?

- Anticipate and then face the tough challenges
- Insist on innovative yet rigorous and pragmatic solutions
- Assemble and train the winning crew

Develop my shore team: Teach the boys to sail

5. Set one-year goals

Target the gold: Begin to develop new procurement process

Win the short race: Deliver Sympix project ahead of expectations

Build a seaworthy boat: Keep TFLS process within cost and cash forecast

How will I do it?

- Accelerate team reconfiguration
- Get buy-in from management for new procurement approach

Invest in my shore team: Take a two-week vacation, no e-mail

6. Map out critical next steps

Assemble the crew: Finalize key hires

Chart the course: Lay the groundwork for Sympix and TFLS projects

How will I do it?

Six months:

- Finalize succession plans
- Set out Sympix timeline

Three months:

- Land a world-class replacement for Jim
- Schedule "action windows" to focus with no e-mail

30 days:

- Bring Alex in Shanghai on board
- Agree on TFLS metrics
- Conduct one-day Sympix offsite

Reconnect with my shore team: Be more present with Jill and the boys

7. Examine key relationships

Sarah, HR manager

Jill, manager of my "shore team"

that understanding what motivates us dramatically increases our ability to achieve big goals.

Next, Richard addresses his **three- to five-year goals** using the language of his purpose statement. We find that this is a good time frame to target first; several years is long enough that even the most disillusioned managers could imagine they'd actually be living into their purpose by then. But it's not so distant that it creates complacency. A goal might be to land a top job—in Richard's case, a global procurement role—but the focus should be on how you will do it, what kind of leader you'll be.

Then he considers **two-year goals**. This is a time frame in which the grand future and current reality begin to merge. What new responsibilities will you take on? What do you have to do to set yourself up for the longer term? Remember to address your personal life, too, because you should be more fully living into your purpose everywhere. Richard's goals explicitly reference his family, or "shore team."

The fifth step—setting **one-year goals**—is often the most challenging. Many people ask, "What if most of what I am doing today isn't aligned in any way with my leadership purpose? How do I get from here to there?" We've found two ways to address this problem. First, think about whether you can rewrite the narrative on parts of your work, or change the way you do some tasks, so that they become an expression of your purpose. For example, the phrase "seaworthy boat" helps Richard see the meaning in managing a basic procurement process. Second, consider whether you can add an activity that is 100% aligned with your purpose. We've found that most people can manage to devote 5% to 10% of their time to something that energizes them and helps others see their strengths. Take Richard's decision to contribute to the global strategic procurement effort: It's not part of his "day job," but it gets him involved in a more purpose-driven project.

Now we get to the nitty-gritty. What are the **critical next steps** that you must take in the coming six months, three months, and 30 days to accomplish the one-year goals you've set out? The importance of small wins is well documented in almost every management discipline from change initiatives to innovation. In detailing your next steps, don't write down all the requirements of your job. List the activities or results that are most critical given your newly clarified leadership purpose and ambitions. You'll probably notice that a number of your tasks seem much less urgent than they did before, while others you had pushed to the side take priority.

Finally, we look at the **key relationships** needed to turn your plan into reality. Identify two or three people who can help you live more fully into your leadership purpose. For Richard, it is Sarah, the HR manager who will help him assemble his crew, and his wife, Jill, the manager of his "shore team."

Executives tell us that their individual purpose-to-impact plans help them stay true to their short- and long-term goals, inspiring courage, commitment, and focus. When they're frustrated or flagging, they pull out the plans to remind themselves what they want to accomplish and how they'll succeed. After creating his plan, the retail operations chief facing global competition said he's no longer "shying away from things that are too hard." Dolf van den Brink said: "I'm much clearer on where I really can contribute and where not. I have full clarity on the kind of roles I aspire to and can make explicit choices along the way."

What creates the greatest leaders and companies? Each of them operates from a slightly different set of assumptions about the world, their industry, what can or can't be done. That individual perspective allows them to create great value and have significant impact. They all operate with a unique leadership purpose. To be a truly effective leader, you must do the same. Clarify your purpose, and put it to work.

Originally published in May 2014. Reprint R1405H

Learning to Learn

by Erika Andersen

ORGANIZATIONS TODAY ARE IN CONSTANT FLUX. Industries are consolidating, new business models are emerging, new technologies are being developed, and consumer behaviors are evolving. For executives, the ever-increasing pace of change can be especially demanding. It forces them to understand and quickly respond to big shifts in the way companies operate and how work must get done. In the words of Arie de Geus, a business theorist, "The ability to learn faster than your competitors may be the only sustainable competitive advantage."

I'm not talking about relaxed armchair or even structured classroom learning. I'm talking about resisting the bias against doing new things, scanning the horizon for growth opportunities, and pushing yourself to acquire radically different capabilities—while still performing your job. That requires a willingness to experiment and become a novice again and again: an extremely discomforting notion for most of us.

Over decades of coaching and consulting to thousands of executives in a variety of industries, however, my colleagues and I have come across people who succeed at this kind of learning. We've identified four attributes they have in spades: aspiration, self-awareness, curiosity, and vulnerability. They truly want to understand and master new skills; they see themselves very clearly; they constantly think of and ask good questions; and they tolerate their own mistakes as they move up the learning curve.

Of course, these things come more naturally to some people than to others. But, drawing on research in psychology and management as well as our work with clients, we have identified some fairly simple mental tools anyone can develop to boost all four attributes—even those that are often considered fixed (aspiration, curiosity, and vulnerability).

Aspiration

It's easy to see aspiration as either there or not: You want to learn a new skill or you don't; you have ambition and motivation or you lack them. But great learners can raise their aspiration level—and that's key, because everyone is guilty of sometimes resisting development that is critical to success.

Think about the last time your company adopted a new approach—overhauled a reporting system, replaced a CRM platform, revamped the supply chain. Were you eager to go along? I doubt it. Your initial response was probably to justify not learning. (*It will take too long. The old way works just fine for me. I bet it's just a flash in the pan.*) When confronted with new learning, this is often our first roadblock: We focus on the negative and unconsciously reinforce our lack of aspiration.

When we *do* want to learn something, we focus on the positive—what we'll gain from learning it—and envision a happy future in which we're reaping those rewards. That propels us into action. Researchers have found that shifting your focus from challenges to benefits is a good way to increase your aspiration to do initially unappealing things. For example, when Nicole Detling, a psychologist at the University of Utah, encouraged aerialists and speed skaters to picture themselves benefiting from a particular skill, they were much more motivated to practice it.

A few years ago I coached a CMO who was hesitant to learn about big data. Even though most of his peers were becoming converts, he'd convinced himself that he didn't have the time to get into it and that it wouldn't be that important to his industry. I finally realized

Idea in Brief

The ever-increasing pace of change in today's organizations requires that executives understand and then quickly respond to constant shifts in how their businesses operate and how work must get done. That means you must resist your innate biases against doing new things in new ways, scan the horizon for growth opportunities, and push yourself to acquire drastically different capabilities—while still doing your existing job. To succeed, you must be willing to experiment and become a novice over and over again, which for most of us is an extremely discomforting proposition.

Over decades of work with managers, the author has found that people who do succeed at this kind of learning have four well-developed attributes: aspiration, self-awareness, curiosity, and vulnerability. They have a deep desire to understand and master new skills; they see themselves very clearly; they're constantly thinking of and asking good questions; and they tolerate their own mistakes as they move up the curve. Andersen has identified some fairly simple mental strategies that anyone can use to boost these attributes.

that this was an aspiration problem and encouraged him to think of ways that getting up to speed on data-driven marketing could help him personally. He acknowledged that it would be useful to know more about how various segments of his customer base were responding to his team's online advertising and in-store marketing campaigns. I then invited him to imagine the situation he'd be in a year later if he was getting that data. He started to show some excitement, saying, "We would be testing different approaches simultaneously, both in-store and online; we'd have good, solid information about which ones were working and for whom; and we could save a lot of time and money by jettisoning the less effective approaches faster." I could almost feel his aspiration rising. Within a few months he'd hired a data analytics expert, made a point of learning from her on a daily basis, and begun to rethink key campaigns in light of his new perspective and skills.

Self-Awareness

Over the past decade or so, most leaders have grown familiar with the concept of self-awareness. They understand that they need to solicit feedback and recognize how others see them. But when it comes to the need for learning, our assessments of ourselves—what we know and don't know, skills we have and don't have—can still be woefully inaccurate. In one study conducted by David Dunning, a Cornell University psychologist, 94% of college professors reported that they were doing "above average work." Clearly, almost half were wrong—many extremely so—and their self-deception surely diminished any appetite for development. Only 6% of respondents saw themselves as having a lot to learn about being an effective teacher.

In my work I've found that the people who evaluate themselves most accurately start the process inside their own heads: They accept that their perspective is often biased or flawed and then strive for greater objectivity, which leaves them much more open to hearing and acting on others' opinions. The trick is to pay attention to how you talk to yourself about yourself and then question the validity of that "self-talk."

Let's say your boss has told you that your team isn't strong enough and that you need to get better at assessing and developing talent. Your initial reaction might be something like *What? She's wrong. My team is strong.* Most of us respond defensively to that sort of criticism. But as soon as you recognize what you're thinking, ask yourself, *Is that accurate? What facts do I have to support it?* In the process of reflection you may discover that you're wrong and your boss is right, or that the truth lies somewhere in between—you cover for some of your reports by doing things yourself, and one of them is inconsistent in meeting deadlines; however, two others are stars. Your inner voice is most useful when it reports the facts of a situation in this balanced way. It should serve as a "fair witness" so that you're open to seeing the areas in which you could improve and how to do so.

One CEO I know was convinced that he was a great manager and leader. He did have tremendous industry knowledge and great

Changing your inner narrative

Unsupportive self-talk	Supportive self-talk
I don't need to learn this.	What would my future look like if I did?
I'm already fine at this.	Am I really? How do I compare with my peers?
This is boring.	I wonder why others find it interesting.
I'm terrible at this.	I'm making beginner mistakes, but I'll get better.

instincts about growing his business, and his board acknowledged those strengths. But he listened only to people who affirmed his view of himself and dismissed input about shortcomings; his team didn't feel engaged or inspired. When he finally started to question his assumptions (*Is everyone on my team focused and productive? If not, is there something I could be doing differently?*), he became much more aware of his developmental needs and open to feedback. He realized that it wasn't enough to have strategic insights; he had to share them with his reports and invite discussion, and then set clear priorities—backed by quarterly team and individual goals, regular progress checks, and troubleshooting sessions.

Curiosity

Kids are relentless in their urge to learn and master. As John Medina writes in *Brain Rules,* "This need for explanation is so powerfully stitched into their experience that some scientists describe it as a drive, just as hunger and thirst and sex are drives." Curiosity is what makes us try something until we can do it, or think about something until we understand it. Great learners retain this childhood drive, or regain it through another application of self-talk. Instead of focusing on and reinforcing initial disinterest in a new subject, they learn to ask themselves "curious questions" about it and follow those questions up with actions. Carol Sansone, a psychology researcher, has found, for example, that people can increase their willingness to tackle necessary tasks by thinking about how they could do the work differently to make it more interesting. In other words, they change their self-talk from *This is boring* to *I wonder if I could . . . ?*

You can employ the same strategy in your working life by noticing the language you use in thinking about things that already interest you—*How . . . ? Why . . . ? I wonder . . . ?*—and drawing on it when you need to become curious. Then take just one step to answer a question you've asked yourself: Read an article, query an expert, find a teacher, join a group—whatever feels easiest.

I recently worked with a corporate lawyer whose firm had offered her a bigger job that required knowledge of employment law—an area she regarded as "the single most boring aspect of the legal profession." Rather than trying to persuade her otherwise, I asked her what she was curious about and why. "Swing dancing," she said. "I'm fascinated by the history of it. I wonder how it developed, and whether it was a response to the Depression—it's such a happy art form. I watch great dancers and think about why they do certain things."

I explained that her "curious language" could be applied to employment law. "I wonder how anyone could find it interesting?" she said jokingly. I told her that was actually an OK place to start. She began thinking out loud about possible answers ("Maybe some lawyers see it as a way to protect both their employees and their companies . . .") and then proposed a few other curious questions ("How might knowing more about this make me a better lawyer?").

Soon she was intrigued enough to connect with a colleague who was experienced in employment law. She asked him what he found interesting about it and how he had acquired his knowledge, and his answers prompted other questions. Over the following months she learned what she needed to know for that aspect of her new role.

The next time you're asked to learn something at the office, or sense that you should because colleagues are doing so, encourage yourself to ask and answer a few curious questions about it—*Why are others so excited about this? How might this make my job easier?*—and then seek out the answers. You'll need to find just one thing about a "boring" topic that sparks your curiosity.

Vulnerability

Once we become good or even excellent at some things, we rarely want to go back to being *not* good at other things. Yes, we're now taught to embrace experimentation and "fast failure" at work. But we're also taught to play to our strengths. So the idea of being bad at something for weeks or months; feeling awkward and slow; having to ask "dumb," "I-don't-know-what-you're-talking-about" questions; and needing step-by-step guidance again and again is extremely scary. Great learners allow themselves to be vulnerable enough to accept that beginner state. In fact, they become reasonably comfortable in it—by managing their self-talk.

Generally, when we're trying something new and doing badly at it, we think terrible thoughts: *I hate this. I'm such an idiot. I'll never get this right. This is so frustrating!* That static in our brains leaves little bandwidth for learning. The ideal mindset for a beginner is both vulnerable and balanced: *I'm going to be bad at this to start with, because I've never done it before. AND I know I can learn to do it over time.* In fact, the researchers Robert Wood and Albert Bandura found in the late 1980s that when people are encouraged to expect mistakes and learn from them early in the process of acquiring new skills, the result is "heightened interest, persistence, and better performance."

I know a senior sales manager from the United States who was recently tapped to run the Asia-Pacific region for his company. He was having a hard time acclimating to living overseas and working with colleagues from other cultures, and he responded by leaning on his sales expertise rather than acknowledging his beginner status in the new environment. I helped him recognize his resistance to being a cultural novice, and he was able to shift his self-talk from *This is so uncomfortable—I'll just focus on what I already know* to *I have a lot to learn about Asian cultures. I'm a quick study, so I'll be able to pick it up*. He told me it was an immediate relief: Simply acknowledging his novice status made him feel less foolish and more relaxed. He started asking the necessary questions, and soon he was seen as open, interested, and beginning to understand his new environment.

———————

The ability to acquire new skills and knowledge quickly and continually is crucial to success in a world of rapid change. If you don't currently have the aspiration, self-awareness, curiosity, and vulnerability to be an effective learner, these simple tools can help you get there.

Originally published in March 2016. Reprint R1603J

Making Yourself Indispensable

by John H. Zenger, Joseph R. Folkman, and Scott K. Edinger

A MANAGER WE'LL call Tom was a midlevel sales executive at a *Fortune* 500 company. After a dozen or so years there, he was thriving—he made his numbers, he was well liked, he got consistently positive reviews. He applied for a promotion that would put him in charge of a high-profile worldwide product-alignment initiative, confident that he was the top candidate and that this was the logical next move for him, a seemingly perfect fit for his skills and ambitions. His track record was solid. He'd made no stupid mistakes or career-limiting moves, and he'd had no run-ins with upper management. He was stunned, then, when a colleague with less experience got the job. What was the matter?

As far as Tom could tell, nothing. Everyone was happy with his work, his manager assured him, and a recent 360-degree assessment confirmed her view. Tom was at or above the norm in every area, strong not only in delivering results but also in problem solving, strategic thinking, and inspiring others to top performance. "No need to reinvent yourself," she said. "Just keep doing what you're doing. Go with your strengths."

But how? Tom was at a loss. Should he think more strategically? Become even more inspiring? Practice problem solving more intently?

It's pretty easy and straightforward to improve on a weakness; you can get steady, measurable results through linear development—that is, by learning and practicing basic techniques. But the data from our decades of work with tens of thousands of executives all over the world has shown us that developing strengths is very different. Doing more of what you already do well yields only incremental improvement. To get appreciably better at it, you have to work on complementary skills—what we call *nonlinear* development. This has long been familiar to athletes as cross-training. A novice runner, for example, benefits from doing stretching exercises and running a few times a week, gradually increasing mileage to build up endurance and muscle memory. But an experienced marathoner won't get significantly faster merely by running ever longer distances. To reach the next level, he needs to supplement that regimen by building up complementary skills through weight training, swimming, bicycling, interval training, yoga, and the like.

So it is with leadership competencies. To move from good to much better, you need to engage in the business equivalent of cross-training. If you're technically adept, for instance, delving even more deeply into technical manuals won't get you nearly as far as honing a complementary skill such as communication, which will make your expertise more apparent and accessible to your coworkers.

In this article we provide a simple guide to becoming a far more effective leader. We will see how Tom identified his strengths, decided which one to focus on and which complementary skill to develop, and what the results were. The process is straightforward, but complements are not always obvious. So first we'll take a closer look at the leadership equivalent of cross-training.

The Interaction Effect

In cross-training, the combination of two activities produces an improvement—an *interaction effect*—substantially greater than either one can produce on its own. There's nothing mysterious here. Combining diet with exercise, for example, has long been known to be substantially more effective in losing weight than either diet or exercise alone.

Idea in Brief

Good leaders can become exceptional by developing just a few of their strengths to the highest level—but not by merely doing more of the same.

Instead, they need to engage in the business equivalent of cross-training—that is, to enhance complementary skills that will enable them to make fuller use of their strengths.

For example, technical skills can become more effective when communication skills improve, making a leader's expertise more apparent and more accessible.

Once a few of their strengths have reached the level of outstanding, leaders become indispensable to their organizations despite the weaknesses they may have.

In our previous research we found 16 differentiating leadership competencies that correlate strongly with positive business outcomes such as increased profitability, employee engagement, revenue, and customer satisfaction. Among those 16, we wondered, could we find pairs that would produce significant interaction effects?

We searched through our database of more than a quarter million 360-degree surveys of some 30,000 developing leaders for pairings that resulted in far higher scores on overall leadership effectiveness than either attribute did on its own. The results were unambiguous. Take, for example, the competencies "focuses on results" and "builds relationships." Only 14% of leaders who were reasonably strong (that is, scored in the 75th percentile) in focusing on results but less so in building relationships reached the extraordinary leadership level: the 90th percentile in overall leadership effectiveness. Similarly, only 12% of those who were reasonably strong in building relationships but less so in focusing on results reached that level. But when an individual performed well in both categories, something dramatic happened: Fully 72% of those in the 75th percentile in both categories reached the 90th percentile in overall leadership effectiveness.

We measured the degree of correlation between overall leadership effectiveness and all possible pairings of our 16 differentiating competencies to learn which pairings were the most powerful. We also matched our 16 competencies with other leadership skills and measured how those pairs correlated with overall leadership effectiveness. We discovered that each of the 16 has up to a dozen associated behaviors—which we call *competency companions*—that were highly correlated with leadership excellence when combined with the differentiating competency. (For a complete list of the competencies and their companions, see the exhibit "What skills will magnify my strengths?")

Consider the main competency "displays honesty and integrity." How would a leader go about improving a relative strength in this area? By being more honest? (We've heard that answer to the question many times.) That's not particularly useful advice. If an executive were weak in this area, we could recommend various ways to improve: Behave more consistently, avoid saying one thing and doing another, follow through on stated commitments, and so on. But a leader with high integrity is most likely already doing those things.

Our competency-companion research suggests a practical path forward. For example, assertiveness is among the behaviors that when paired with honesty and integrity correlate most strongly with high levels of overall leadership effectiveness. We don't mean to imply a causal relationship here: Assertiveness doesn't make someone honest, and integrity doesn't produce assertiveness. But if a highly principled leader learned to become more assertive, he might be more likely to speak up and act with the courage of his convictions, thus applying his strength more widely or frequently to become a more effective leader.

Our data suggest other ways in which a competency companion can reinforce a leadership strength. It might make the strength more apparent, as in the case of the technically strong leader who improves her ability to communicate. Or skills learned in developing the competency companion might be profitably applied to the main competency. A leader strong in innovativeness, for instance, might learn how to champion change, thus encouraging his team to achieve results in new and more creative ways.

What skills will magnify my strengths?

Our research shows that 16 leadership competencies correlate strongly with positive business outcomes. Each of them has up to a dozen "competency companions" whose development will strengthen the core skill.

Character

Displays honesty and integrity

- Shows concern and consideration for others
- Is trustworthy
- Demonstrates optimism
- Is assertive
- Inspires and motivates others
- Deals well with ambiguity
- Is decisive
- Focuses on results

Personal capability

Exhibits technical/professional expertise

- Solves problems and analyzes issues
- Builds relationships and networks
- Communicates powerfully and broadly
- Pursues excellence
- Takes initiative
- Develops others
- Displays honesty and integrity
- Acts in the team's best interest

Solves problems and analyzes issues

- Takes initiative
- Is organized and good at planning
- Is decisive
- Innovates
- Wants to tackle challenges
- Develops strategic perspective
- Acts independently
- Has technical expertise
- Communicates powerfully and broadly

Innovates

- Is willing to take risks and challenge the status quo
- Supports others in risk-taking
- Solves problems and analyzes issues
- Champions change
- Learns quickly from success and failure
- Develops strategic perspective
- Takes initiative

Practices self-development

- Listens
- Is open to others' ideas

- Respects others
- Displays honesty and integrity
- Inspires and motivates others
- Provides effective feedback and development
- Takes initiative
- Is willing to take risks and challenge the status quo

Getting results

Focuses on results

- Is organized and good at planning
- Displays honesty and integrity
- Anticipates problems
- Sees desired results clearly
- Provides effective feedback and development
- Establishes stretch goals
- Is personally accountable
- Is quick to act
- Provides rewards and recognition
- Creates a high-performance team
- Marshals adequate resources
- Innovates

Establishes stretch goals

- Inspires and motivates others
- Is willing to take risks and challenge the status quo
- Gains the support of others
- Develops strategic perspective
- Champions change
- Is decisive
- Has technical and business expertise
- Focuses on results

Takes initiative

- Anticipates problems
- Emphasizes speed
- Is organized and good at planning
- Champions others
- Deals well with ambiguity
- Follows through
- Inspires and motivates others
- Establishes stretch goals
- Displays honesty and integrity

(continued)

What skills will magnify my strengths?   (*continued*)

Interpersonal skills

Communicates powerfully and broadly

- Inspires and motivates others
- Develops strategic perspective
- Establishes stretch goals
- Deals effectively with the outside world
- Is trustworthy
- Involves others
- Translates messages for clarity
- Solves problems and analyzes issues
- Takes initiative
- Innovates
- Develops others

Inspires and motivates others

- Connects emotionally with others
- Establishes stretch goals
- Exhibits clear vision and direction
- Communicates powerfully and broadly
- Develops others
- Collaborates and fosters teamwork
- Nurtures innovation
- Takes initiative
- Champions change
- Is a strong role model

Builds relationships

- Collaborates and fosters teamwork
- Displays honesty and integrity
- Develops others
- Listens
- Communicates powerfully and broadly
- Provides rewards and recognition
- Practices inclusion and values diversity
- Demonstrates optimism
- Practices self-development

Develops others

- Practices self-development
- Shows concern and consideration for others
- Is motivated by the success of others
- Practices inclusion and values diversity
- Develops strategic perspective
- Provides effective feedback and development
- Inspires and motivates others

- Innovates
- Provides rewards and recognition
- Displays honesty and integrity

Collaborates and fosters teamwork

- Is trustworthy
- Builds relationships and networks
- Practices inclusion and values diversity
- Develops strategic perspective
- Establishes stretch goals
- Communicates powerfully and broadly
- Displays honesty and integrity
- Adapts to change
- Inspires and motivates others
- Develops others

Leading change

Develops strategic perspective

- Focuses on customers
- Innovates
- Solves problems and analyzes issues
- Communicates powerfully and broadly
- Establishes stretch goals
- Demonstrates business acumen
- Champions change
- Inspires and motivates others

Champions change

- Inspires and motivates others
- Builds relationships and networks
- Develops others
- Provides rewards and recognition
- Practices inclusion and values diversity
- Innovates
- Focuses on results
- Is willing to take risks and challenge the status quo
- Develops strategic perspective

Connects the group to the outside world

- Develops broad perspective
- Develops strategic perspective
- Inspires and motivates others
- Has strong interpersonal skills
- Takes initiative
- Gathers and assimilates information
- Champions change
- Communicates powerfully and broadly

Building Strengths, Step by Step

As a practical matter, cross-training for leadership skills is clear-cut: (1) Identify your strengths. (2) Choose a strength to focus on according to its importance to the organization and how passionately you feel about it. (3) Select a complementary behavior you'd like to enhance. (4) Develop it in a linear way.

Identify your strengths

Strengths can arguably be identified in a variety of ways. But we contend that in the context of effective leadership, your view of your own (or even some perfectly objective view, supposing one could be had) is less important than other people's, because leadership is all about your effect on others. That's why we start with a 360—as Tom did.

Ideally, you should go about this in a psychometrically valid way, through a formal process in which you and your direct reports, peers, and bosses anonymously complete questionnaires ranking your leadership attributes on a quantitative scale. You and they should also answer some qualitative, open-ended questions concerning your strengths, your fatal flaws (if any), and the relative importance of those attributes to the company. By "fatal flaws," we mean flaws so critical that they can overpower any strengths you have or may develop—flaws that can derail your career.

Not every organization is able or willing to conduct 360s for everyone. So if that's not feasible, you may be able to solicit qualitative data from your colleagues if—and this is a big caveat—you can make them feel comfortable enough to be honest in their feedback. You could create your own feedback form and ask people to return it anonymously. (See the sidebar "An Informal 360" for a suggested set of questions.) We have also seen earnest one-on-one conversations work for this purpose; if nothing else, they show your coworkers that you are genuinely interested in self-improvement. (Nevertheless, it's unlikely that anyone will tell you directly if you have fatal flaws.)

In interpreting the results, people commonly focus first on their lowest scores. But unless those are extremely low (in the 10th percentile),

An Informal 360

BEFORE YOU CAN BUILD ON YOUR STRENGTHS, you need an objective view of what they are. Ideally, this comes from a formal, confidential 360-degree evaluation. But if that's not possible, a direct approach can work. Try simply asking your team members, colleagues, and boss these simple questions, either in person or in writing.

- What leadership skills do you think are strengths for me?

- Is there anything I do that might be considered a fatal flaw—that could derail my career or lead me to fail in my current job if it's not addressed?

- What leadership ability, if outstanding, would have the most significant impact on the productivity or effectiveness of the organization?

- What leadership abilities of mine have the most significant impact on you?

Do your best to exhibit receptiveness and to create a feeling of safety (especially for direct reports). Make it clear that you're seeking self-improvement. Tell your colleagues explicitly that you are open to negative feedback and that you will absorb it professionally and appropriately—and without retribution. Of course, you need to follow through on this promise, or the entire process will fail.

---

that's a mistake. (We have found that 20% of executives do typically discover such a critical problem in their 360s; if you're among them, you must fix the flaw, which you can do in a linear way.)

What makes leaders indispensable to their organizations, our data unmistakably show, is not being good at many things but being uniquely outstanding at a few things. Such strengths allow a leader's inevitable weaknesses to be overlooked. The executives in our database who exhibited no profound (that is, in the 90th percentile) strengths scored only in the 34th percentile, on average, in overall leadership effectiveness. But if they had just one outstanding strength, their overall leadership effectiveness score rose to the 64th percentile, on average. In other words, the difference between being in the bottom third of leaders and being almost in the top third is a single extraordinary strength. Two profound strengths put leaders close to the top quartile, three put them in the top quintile, and four

What difference can a single strength make?

Raising just one competency to the level of outstanding can up your overall leadership effectiveness ranking from the bottom third to almost the top third.

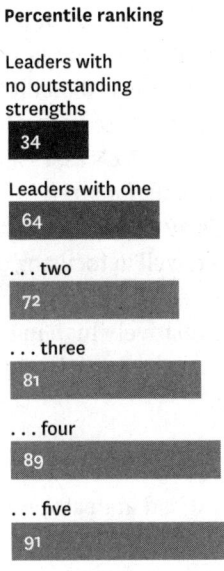

Percentile ranking

Leaders with
no outstanding
strengths
34

Leaders with one
64

. . . two
72

. . . three
81

. . . four
89

. . . five
91

put them nearly in the top decile. (See the exhibit "What difference can a single strength make?")

In this context, a look at Tom's 360 results sheds light on the question of why he was passed over for a plum assignment. Tom had no critical flaws, but he hadn't yet demonstrated any outstanding strengths either. With no strengths above the 70th percentile, he didn't score "good," let alone "outstanding," in overall leadership ability. Anyone in the organization with a single notable strength was likely to outpace him for promotion opportunities. But if Tom could lift just a few of his relative strengths from the 70th to the 80th and then the 90th percentile, his overall leadership effectiveness might go from above average to good to exceptional. Clearly, those strengths merited a closer examination.

Like many people, though, Tom was initially galvanized by the low bars on his chart, which evoked a mixture of guilt and denial. His relatively low score on building relationships called up uncomfortable memories of high school—something he didn't mention as he looked over the results with his boss. But he did say that he couldn't believe he wasn't scored higher on innovativeness, and he started to tick off initiatives he felt he deserved credit for. Maybe he was innovative, and maybe he wasn't. It's common for your self-assessment to vary sharply from everyone else's assessment of you. But remember that it's others' opinions that matter.

When Tom did turn his attention to his strengths, he wasn't surprised to see that he scored well in focusing on results and in solving problems and analyzing issues. Less obvious to him, and perhaps more gratifying, were his relatively high marks in developing strategic perspective and inspiring and motivating others. Now he could move on to the next step.

Choose a strength to focus on

Choices between good and bad are easy. But choices between good and good cause us to deliberate and second-guess. It may not matter which competency Tom selected, since enhancing any one of them would markedly improve his leadership effectiveness. Nevertheless, we recommend that developing leaders focus on a competency that matters to the organization and about which they feel some passion, because a strength you feel passionate about that is not important to your organization is essentially a hobby, and a strength the organization needs that you don't feel passionate about is just a chore.

You can use your colleagues' importance ratings from the 360 assessment to get a somewhat objective view of organizational needs. But the prospect of following his passions alarmed Tom, who didn't know how to begin. Answering a series of questions made the notion more concrete. For each of the 16 competencies, he ran down the following list:

- Do I look for ways to enhance this skill?
- Do I look for new ways to use it?

- Am I energized, not exhausted, when I use it?

- Do I pursue projects in which I can apply this strength?

- Can I imagine devoting time to improving it?

- Would I enjoy getting better at this skill?

Counting his "yes" answers gave Tom a solid way to quantify his passions. A simple worksheet showed him how his skills, his passions, and the organization's needs dovetailed (see the exhibit "Narrowing down the options"). When Tom checked off his top five competencies, his five passions, and the organization's top priorities, he could see a clear convergence. He decided to focus on the strength that, as it happens, we have found to be most universally associated with extraordinary leadership: "inspires and motivates others."

Select a complementary behavior

People who excel at motivating others are good at persuading them to take action and to go the extra mile. They effectively exercise power to influence key decisions for the benefit of the organization. They know how to motivate different people in different ways. So it was not surprising that Tom already did those things pretty well. He scanned the list of competency companions:

- Connects emotionally with others

- Establishes stretch goals

- Exhibits clear vision and direction

- Communicates powerfully and broadly

- Develops others

- Collaborates and fosters teamwork

- Nurtures innovation

- Takes initiative

- Champions change

- Is a strong role model

Narrowing down the options

The strength you focus on should be both important to the organization and important to you. A simple worksheet (like Tom's, below) can help you see where your strengths and interests and the needs of your organization converge. Choose five competencies in each of the three categories.

	Your competencies	Your passions	Organizational needs	Total
1. Displays honesty and integrity				
2. Exhibits technical/professional expertise	X			1
3. Solves problems and analyzes issues	X			1
4. Innovates		X	X	2
5. Practices self-development				
6. Focuses on results	X			1
7. Establishes stretch goals				
8. Takes initiative		X		1
9. Communicates powerfully and broadly			X	1
10. Inspires and motivates others	X	X	X	(3)
11. Builds relationships			X	1
12. Develops others		X		1
13. Collaborates and fosters teamwork		X		1
14. Develops strategic perspective	X		X	2
15. Champions change				
16. Connects the group to the outside world				

You should choose a companion behavior that, like a good strength, is important to the organization and makes you feel enthusiastic about tackling it. But at this point it's also constructive to consider your lower scores. In talking these points over with his manager, Tom decided to work on his communication skills, which didn't score particularly high but were high enough that raising them a little could make a significant difference.

Develop it in a linear way

Having settled on a competency companion, Tom could now work at directly improving his basic skills in that area. Strong communicators speak concisely and deliver effective presentations. Their instructions are clear. They write well. They can explain new concepts clearly. They help people understand how their work contributes to broader business objectives. They can translate terms used by people in different functions. Tom saw lots of room for improvement here: No one would ever call him concise; he didn't always finish sentences he'd started; and he found writing a challenge.

We would have recommended that he look for as many opportunities as possible, both inside and outside work, to improve his communication. He could take a course in business writing. He could practice with friends and family, in his church or his community. He could volunteer to make presentations to senior management or ask colleagues to critique some of his memos and e-mails. He might volunteer to help high school students write college application essays. He could videotape himself making speeches or join a local Toastmasters club.

Tom decided to seek the advice of a colleague whose communication skills he admired. The colleague suggested (among other things) that because writing was not a strong point, Tom should practice communicating more in person or over the phone. This turned out to be challenging: Tom found that before he could even begin, he had to change his approach to e-mail, because he was in the habit of constantly checking and replying to it throughout the day. He couldn't always substitute the phone, because he couldn't make calls while he was in a meeting or talking to someone else. He started to set aside specific times of the day for e-mail so that he could reply by phone or in person—a small change that had unexpected consequences. Instead of being interrupted and distracted at random moments throughout the day (and evening), his staffers had concentrated, direct interactions with him. They found these more efficient and effective, even though they could no longer choose when (or whether) to reply to Tom's cryptic e-mails. Tom found that he connected better with people he talked to, both because his attention wasn't divided between them and his BlackBerry and because he could read their tone of voice and body language. As a result, he absorbed more information, and his colleagues felt he was more attentive to their views.

Tom also started to pay more attention not just to how he was communicating but to what he was saying. His colleague suggested that Tom start to keep track of how often he issued instructions versus how often he asked questions. Tom also took note of how much of what he said was criticism (constructive or otherwise) and how much was encouragement. Increasing the proportion of questions and encouragement had an immediate effect: His team began to understand him more quickly, so he didn't have to repeat himself as often. Several team members actually thanked him for allowing them to express their points of view.

Like Tom, you should expect to see some concrete evidence of improvement within 30 to 60 days. If you don't, what you're doing is not working. That said, complementary behaviors improve steadily with practice, and Tom's progress is typical: Fifteen months later, on taking another 360, he found he'd moved into the 82nd percentile in his ability to inspire. He wasn't extraordinary yet, but he was getting close. Our advice would be to keep at it—to improve another competency companion or two until he reaches the 90th percentile and becomes truly exceptional at inspiring others. Then he can start the entire process again with another strength and its complements, and another—at which point he will be making a uniquely valuable contribution to his company.

Can You Overdo It?

Everyone knows someone who is too assertive, too technically oriented, too focused on driving for results. Many people cite examples like these to argue against the wisdom of improving your leadership effectiveness by strengthening your strengths. Our research does in fact show a point where balance becomes important. The data suggest that the difference between having four profound strengths and having five is a gain of merely 2 percentage points in overall leadership effectiveness. Thus leaders who are already exceptional should consider one more variable.

You will note in the exhibit "What skills will magnify my strengths?" that the 16 differentiating competencies fall into five broader categories: character, personal capability, getting results, interpersonal skills, and leading change. People who have many strengths should consider how they are distributed across those categories and focus improvement efforts on an underrepresented one.

But we cannot think of a less constructive approach to improving your leadership effectiveness than treating your strengths as weaknesses. Have you ever known anyone who had too much integrity? Was too effective a communicator? Was just too inspiring? Developing competency companions works precisely because, rather than simply doing more of the same, you are enhancing how you already behave with new ways of working and interacting that will make that behavior more effective.

Focusing on your strengths is hardly a new idea. Forty-four years ago Peter Drucker made the business case eloquently in *The Effective Executive:* "Unless . . . an executive looks for strength and works at making strength productive, he will only get the impact of what a man cannot do, of his lacks, his weaknesses, his impediments to performance and effectiveness. To staff from what there is not and to focus on weakness is wasteful—a misuse, if not abuse, of the human resource." Since then a body of work has grown up supporting and advocating for Drucker's approach. Our own research shows how big a difference developing a few strengths can make. It is distressing to find that fewer than 10% of the executives we work with have any plan to do so.

We are convinced that the problem is less a matter of conviction than of execution. Executives need a path to enhancing their strengths that is as clear as the one to fixing their weaknesses. That is the greatest value, we believe, of the cross-training approach: It allows people to use the linear improvement techniques they know and understand to produce a nonlinear result.

Often executives complain to us that there are not enough good leaders in their organizations. We would argue that in fact far too many leaders are merely good. The challenge is not to replace bad leaders with good ones; it is to turn people like Tom—hardworking, capable executives who are reasonably good at their jobs—into outstanding leaders with distinctive strengths.

Originally published in October 2011. Reprint R1110E

Make Time for the Work That Matters

by Julian Birkinshaw and Jordan Cohen

MORE HOURS IN THE DAY. It's one thing everyone wants, and yet it's impossible to attain. But what if you could free up significant time—maybe as much as 20% of your workday—to focus on the responsibilities that really matter?

We've spent the past three years studying how knowledge workers can become more productive and found that the answer is simple: Eliminate or delegate unimportant tasks and replace them with value-added ones. Our research indicates that knowledge workers spend a great deal of their time—an average of 41%—on discretionary activities that offer little personal satisfaction and could be handled competently by others. So why do they keep doing them? Because ridding oneself of work is easier said than done. We instinctively cling to tasks that make us feel busy and thus important, while our bosses, constantly striving to do more with less, pile on as many responsibilities as we're willing to accept.

We believe there's a way forward, however. Knowledge workers can make themselves more productive by thinking consciously about how they spend their time; deciding which tasks matter most to them and their organizations; and dropping or creatively outsourcing the rest. We tried this intervention with 15 executives at different companies, and they were able to dramatically reduce their involvement in low-value tasks: They cut desk work by an average of six hours a week and meeting time by an average of two hours a week. And the benefits were clear. For example, when Lotta Laitinen, a manager at

If, a Scandinavian insurance broker, jettisoned meetings and administrative tasks in order to spend more time supporting her team, it led to a 5% increase in sales by her unit over a three-week period.

While not everyone in our study was quite that successful, the results still astounded us. By simply asking knowledge workers to rethink and shift the balance of their work, we were able to help them free up nearly a fifth of their time—an average of one full day a week—and focus on more worthwhile tasks with the hours they saved.

Why It's So Hard

Knowledge workers present a real challenge to managers. The work they do is difficult to observe (since a lot of it happens inside their heads), and the quality of it is frequently subjective. A manager may suspect that an employee is spending her time inefficiently but be hard-pressed to diagnose the problem, let alone come up with a solution.

We interviewed 45 knowledge workers in 39 companies across eight industries in the United States and Europe to see how they spent their days. We found that even the most dedicated and impressive performers devoted large amounts of time to tedious, non-value-added activities such as desk work and "managing across" the organization (for example, meetings with people in other departments). These are tasks that the knowledge workers themselves rated as offering little personal utility and low value to the company.

There are many reasons why this happens. Most of us feel entangled in a web of commitments from which it can be painful to extricate ourselves: We worry that we're letting our colleagues or employers down if we stop doing certain tasks. "I want to appear busy and productive—the company values team players," one participant observed. Also, those less important items on our to-do lists are not entirely without benefit. Making progress on any task—even an inessential one—increases our feelings of engagement and satisfaction, research has shown. And although meetings are widely derided as a waste of time, they offer opportunities to socialize and connect with coworkers. "I actually quite look forward to face-to-face meetings," one respondent told us. "A call is more efficient, but it's a cold, lifeless medium."

Idea in Brief

More hours in the day. It's one thing everyone wants, and yet it's impossible to attain. But what if you could free up significant time—maybe as much as 20% of your workday—to focus on the responsibilities that really matter? The authors' research shows that knowledge workers spend, on average, 41% of their time on activities that offer little personal satisfaction and could be handled competently by others.

Knowledge workers can become more productive by thinking consciously about how they spend their time, deciding which tasks matter most to them and their organizations, and dropping or creatively outsourcing the rest.

The tasks to be dropped are sorted into:

- **quick kills** (things you can stop doing now, without any negative effects)

- **off-load opportunities** (work that can be delegated with minimal effort)

- **long-term redesign** (work that needs to be reconceived or restructured)

Once the tasks are disposed of, the freed-up time is spent focusing on more-important work.

When 15 executives tried this, they were able to reduce desk work by an average of six hours per week and meetings by two hours per week. They filled the time with value-added tasks like coaching and strategizing.

Organizations share some of the blame for less-than-optimal productivity. Cost cutting has been prevalent over the past decade, and knowledge workers, like most employees, have had to take on some low-value tasks—such as making travel arrangements—that distract them from more important work. Even though business confidence is rebounding, many companies are hesitant to add back resources, particularly administrative ones. What's more, increasingly complicated regulatory environments and tighter control systems in many industries have contributed to risk-averse corporate cultures that discourage senior people from ceding work to less seasoned colleagues. The consequences are predictable: "My team is understaffed and underskilled, so my calendar is a nightmare and I get pulled into many more meetings than I should," one study subject reported. Another commented, "I face the constraint of the working capacity of the people I delegate to."

The work that knowledge workers do

Our research shows that desk-based work and "managing across" take up two-thirds of knowledge workers' time, on average . . .

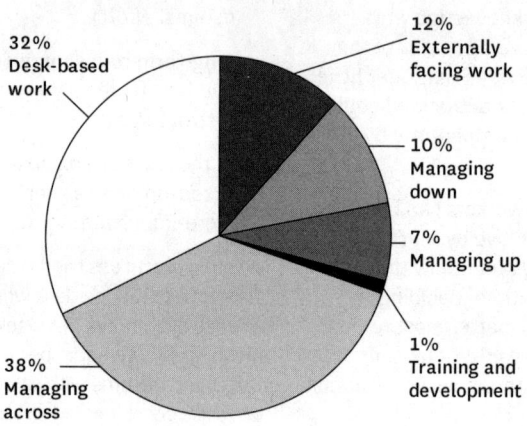

Time spent on activities

32% Desk-based work

12% Externally facing work

10% Managing down

7% Managing up

1% Training and development

38% Managing across

. . . and yet those tasks were rated as most easily off-loaded and tiresome.

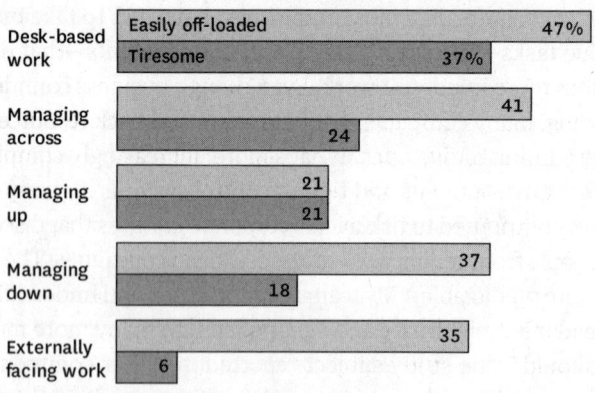

Worth the time?

Desk-based work
- Easily off-loaded 47%
- Tiresome 37%

Managing across
- 41
- 24

Managing up
- 21
- 21

Managing down
- 37
- 18

Externally facing work
- 35
- 6

Armed with this knowledge, study participants dropped, delegated, outsourced, or postponed low-value tasks to free up time for more important work.

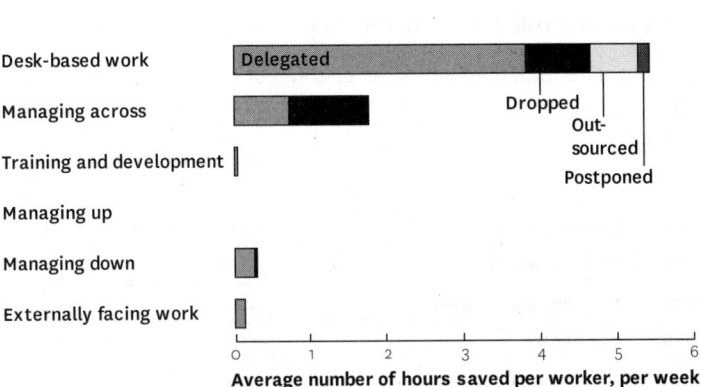

Time saved

Desk-based work — Delegated

Managing across

Training and development — Dropped / Out-sourced / Postponed

Managing up

Managing down

Externally facing work

0   1   2   3   4   5   6

Average number of hours saved per worker, per week

Some companies do try to help their knowledge workers focus on the value-added parts of their job. For example, one of us (Jordan Cohen) helped Pfizer create a service called pfizerWorks, which allows employees to outsource less important tasks. We've also seen corporate initiatives that ban e-mail on Fridays, put time limits on meetings, and forbid internal PowerPoint presentations. But it's very difficult to change institutional norms, and when knowledge workers don't buy in to such top-down directives, they find creative ways to resist or game the system, which only makes matters worse. We propose a sensible middle ground: judicious, self-directed interventions supported by management that help knowledge workers help themselves.

What Workers Can Do

Our process, a variant of the classic Start/Stop/Continue exercise, is designed to help you make small but significant changes to your day-to-day work schedule. We facilitated this exercise with the 15 executives mentioned above, and they achieved some remarkable results.

Self-Assessment:
Identifying Low-Value Tasks

MAKE A LIST OF EVERYTHING YOU DID yesterday or the day before, divided into 30- or 60-minute chunks. For each task, ask yourself four questions:

How valuable is this activity to the firm?

Suppose you're updating your boss or a senior executive on your performance. Would you mention this task? Would you be able to justify spending time on it?

	Score
It contributes in a significant way toward the company's overall objectives	4
It contributes in a small way	3
It has no impact, positive or negative	2
It has a negative impact	1

To what extent could I let this go?

Imagine that because of a family emergency, you arrive at work two hours late and have to prioritize the day's activities. Which category would this activity fall in?

Essential: This takes top priority	4
Important: I need to get this done today	3
Discretionary: I'll get to it if time allows	2
Unimportant/optional: I can cut this immediately	1

How much personal value do I get from doing it?

Imagine that you're financially independent and creating your dream job. Would you keep this task or jettison it?

Identify low-value tasks

Using our self-assessment, look at all your daily activities and decide which ones are (a) not that important to either you or your firm and (b) relatively easy to drop, delegate, or outsource. Our research suggests that at least one-quarter of a typical knowledge worker's

Definitely keep: It's one of the best parts of my job	5
Probably keep: I enjoy this activity	4
Not sure: This task has good and bad points	3
Probably drop: I find this activity somewhat tiresome	2
Definitely jettison: I dislike doing it	1

To what extent could someone else do it on my behalf?

Suppose you've been tapped to handle a critical, fast-track initiative and have to assign some of your work to colleagues for three months. Would you drop, delegate, or keep this task?

Only I (or someone senior to me) can handle this task	5
This task is best done by me because of my particular skill set and other, linked responsibilities	4
If structured properly, this task could be handled satisfactorily by someone junior to me	3
This task could easily be handled by a junior employee or outsourced to a third party	2
This task could be dropped altogether	1

Tally your score

A low total score (10 or lower) reflects a task that is a likely candidate for delegation or elimination.

To see how you stack up and to get advice for improved productivity, go to hbr.org/web/2013/08/assessment/make-time-for-work-that-matters for an interactive assessment tool.

---

activities fall into both categories, so you should aim to find up to 10 hours of time per week. The participants in our study pinpointed a range of expendable tasks. Lotta Laitinen, the manager at If, quickly identified several meetings and routine administrative tasks she could dispense with. Shantanu Kumar, CEO of a small technology company in London, realized he was too involved in project planning details, while Vincent Bryant, a manager at GDF SUEZ Energy Services, was surprised to see how much time he was wasting in sorting documents.

Decide whether to drop, delegate, or redesign

Sort the low-value tasks into three categories: *quick kills* (things you can stop doing now with no negative effects), *off-load opportunities* (tasks that can be delegated with minimal effort), and *long-term redesign* (work that needs to be restructured or overhauled). Our study participants found that this step forced them to reflect carefully on their real contributions to their respective organizations. "I took a step back and asked myself, 'Should I be doing this in the first place? Can my subordinate do it? Is he up to it?'" recalls Johann Barchechath, a manager at BNP Paribas. "This helped me figure out what was valuable for the bank versus what was valuable for me—and what we simply shouldn't have been doing at all." Another participant noted, "I realized that the big change I should make is to say no up-front to low-value tasks and not commit myself in the first place."

Off-load tasks

We heard from many participants that delegation was initially the most challenging part—but ultimately very rewarding. One participant said he couldn't stop worrying about the tasks he had reassigned, while another told us he had trouble remembering "to push, prod, and chase." Barchechath observed, "I learned about the importance of timing in delegating something—it is possible to delegate too early."

Most participants eventually overcame those stumbling blocks. They delegated from 2% to 20% of their work with no decline in their productivity or their team's. "I overestimated my subordinate's capability at first, but it got easier after a while, and even having a partially done piece of work created energy for me," Barchechath said. A bonus was that junior employees benefited from getting more involved. "[She] told me several times that she really appreciated it," he added. Vincent Bryant decided to off-load tasks to a virtual personal assistant and says that although he was concerned about getting up to speed with the service, "it was seamless."

Allocate freed-up time

The goal, of course, is to be not just efficient but effective. So the next step is to determine how to best make use of the time you've saved. Write down two or three things you should be doing but aren't, and then keep a log to assess whether you're using your time more effectively. Some of our study participants were able to go home a bit earlier to enjoy their families (which probably made them happier and more productive the next day). Some unfortunately reported that their time was immediately swallowed up by unforeseen events: "I cleared my in-box and found myself firefighting."

But more than half reclaimed the extra hours to do better work. "For me the most useful part was identifying the important things I don't get time for usually," Kumar said. "I stopped spending time with my project planning tool and instead focused on strategic activities, such as the product road map." Laitinen used her freed-up schedule to listen in on client calls, observe her top salespeople, and coach her employees one-on-one. The result was that stunning three-week sales jump of 5%, with the biggest increases coming from below-average performers. A question naire showed that employee responses to the experiment were positive, and Laitinen found that she missed nothing by dropping some of her work. "The first week was really stressful, because I had to do so much planning, but by the middle of the test period, I was more relaxed, and I was satisfied when I went home every day."

Commit to your plan

Although this process is entirely self-directed, it's crucial to share your plan with a boss, colleague, or mentor. Explain which activities you are getting out of and why. And agree to discuss what you've achieved in a few weeks' time. Without this step, it's all too easy to slide back into bad habits. Many of our participants found that their managers were helpful and supportive. Laitinen's boss, Sven Kärnekull, suggested people to whom she could delegate her work.

Other participants discovered that simply voicing the commitment to another person helped them follow through.

———————

With relatively little effort and no management directive, the small intervention we propose can significantly boost productivity among knowledge workers. Such shifts are not always easy, of course. "It's hard to make these changes without the discipline of someone standing over you," one of our study participants remarked. But all agreed that the exercise was a useful "forcing mechanism" to help them become more efficient, effective, and engaged employees and managers. To do the same, you don't have to redesign any parts of an organization, reengineer a work process, or transform a business model. All you have to do is ask the right questions and act on the answers. After all, if you're a knowledge worker, isn't using your judgment what you were hired for?

Originally published in September 2013. Reprint R1309K

Collaboration without Burnout

by Rob Cross, Scott Taylor, and Deb Zehner

"**SO MANY DIFFERENT** *people can get to you through different channels, and the pressure is enormous.*"

"*Constant e-mail, international travel, calls at all hours—I was exhausted. The collaborative demands eventually wore me down.*"

"*I always felt I had to do more, go further, save the day. I would become people's life raft and then almost drown.*"

These are the voices of collaborative overload.

As organizations become more global, adopt matrixed structures, offer increasingly complex products and services, and enable 24/7 communication, they are requiring employees to collaborate with more internal colleagues and external contacts than ever before. According to research from Connected Commons, most managers now spend 85% or more of their work time on e-mail, in meetings, and on the phone, and the demand for such activities has jumped by 50% over the past decade. Companies benefit, of course: Faster innovation and more-seamless client service are two by-products of greater collaboration. But along with all this comes significantly less time for focused individual work, careful reflection, and sound decision making. A 2016 HBR article coauthored by one of us dubbed this destructive phenomenon *collaborative overload* and suggested ways that organizations might combat it.

Over the past few years we've conducted further research—both quantitative and qualitative—to better understand the problem and uncover solutions that individuals can implement on their own. Working with 20 global organizations in diverse fields (software, consumer products, professional services, manufacturing, and life sciences), we started by creating models of employees' collaborations and considering the effect of those interactions on engagement, performance, and voluntary attrition. We then used network analyses to identify efficient collaborators—people who work productively with a wide variety of others but use the least amount of their own and their colleagues' time—and interviewed 200 of them (100 men and 100 women) about their working lives. We learned a great deal about how overload happens and what leaders must do to avoid it so that they can continue to thrive.

Not surprisingly, we found that always-on work cultures, encroaching technology, demanding bosses, difficult clients, and inefficient coworkers were a big part of the problem, and most of those challenges do require organizational solutions. But we discovered in many cases that external time sinks were matched by another enemy: individuals' own mindsets and habits. Fortunately, people can overcome those obstacles themselves, right away, with some strategic self-management.

We uncovered best practices in three broad categories: *beliefs* (understanding why we take on too much); *role, schedule, and network* (eliminating unnecessary collaboration to make time for work that is aligned with professional aspirations and personal values); and *behavior* (ensuring that necessary or desired collaborative work is as productive as possible). Not all our recommendations will suit everyone: People's needs differ by personality, hierarchical level, and work context. But we found that when the people we studied took action on just four or five of them, they were able to claw back 18% to 24% of their collaborative time.

Two Types of Overload

Collaborative overload generally occurs in either a surge or a slow burn. A surge can result from a promotion, a request from a boss or a colleague to take on or help out with a project, or the desire to jump into

Idea in Brief

As organizations become more global, matrixed, and complex, they are requiring employees to collaborate with more internal colleagues and external contacts than ever before. According to research, most managers now spend 85% or more of their work time on e-mail, in meetings, and on the phone. And although greater collaboration has benefits, it also leaves significantly less time for focused individual work, careful reflection, and sound decision making.

Organizational solutions are, of course, necessary to eradicate collaborative overload across the board. But research shows that with some strategic self-management, individuals can also tackle the problem on their own, clawing back 18% to 24% of their collaborative time.

The first step is to understand why you take on too much work for and with others; this often involves challenging your identity as a "helper," a "team player," or a "star performer." Next, figure out how you add—and from where you derive—the most value and eliminate any collaborations that distract from that work. Last, ensure that the collaboration you continue with is as productive as possible.

an "extracurricular" work activity because you feel obligated or don't want to miss out. Consider Mike, an insurance company executive who was already managing multiple projects—one of which had his entire team working day and night to turn around a struggling segment of the business. When his boss asked him to help create a new unit that would allow the company to present a single face to the market, he felt he couldn't say no. It was a great development opportunity—to which his skills were perfectly suited—and it offered prime exposure to senior management. Yet he couldn't abandon his existing team in the midst of its work. So he decided to do both jobs at once.

A slow burn is more insidious and occurs through incremental increases in the volume, diversity, and pace of collaborative demands over time, as personal effectiveness leads to larger networks and greater scope of responsibilities. Go-to people in organizations suffer from this type of overload. As we gain experience, we often tend to take on more work, and our identities start to become intertwined with accomplishment, helping, or being in the know. We tend not to question what we are doing as we add tasks or work late into the night on e-mail. And, of course, our colleagues welcome these tendencies; as we gain reputations for competence and responsiveness, people in our networks bring us more work and requests. Ellen, an 18-year veteran of a *Fortune* 100 technology company, is a case in point. She was fiercely driven and took pride in her ability to help colleagues, solve problems, and cut through bureaucracy to get things done. Eventually, however, she felt weighed down by a list of projects and commitments that were "beyond the realm of doable."

Though Mike's and Ellen's situations are different, our research suggests that the solutions to their and others' overload problems are similar. They cannot continue to work the same way they always have and remain effective. They need to take better charge of their working lives.

Why We Take On Too Much

The first step in combating collaborative overload is to recognize how much of it is driven by your own desire to maintain a reputation as a helpful, knowledgeable, or influential colleague or to avoid the anxiety that stems from ceding control over or declining to participate in group work. For example, someone who engages in the entire life cycle of a small project, beyond the time when the need for her expertise has passed, might pride herself on supporting teammates and ensuring a high-quality result. But that's not the kind of collaboration that makes a difference over the long term; indeed, too much of it will prevent her from doing more important work.

Knowing why you accept collaborative work—above and beyond what your manager and your company demand—is how you begin to combat overload. When we counsel executives, we ask them to reflect on the specific identity-based triggers that most often lead them into overload. For example: Do you crave the feeling of accomplishment that comes from ticking less challenging items off your to-do list? Does your ambition to be influential or recognized for your expertise cause you to attend meetings or discussions that don't truly require your involvement? Do you pride yourself on being always ready to answer questions and pitch in on group work? Do you agree to take on collaborative activities because you're worried about being labeled a poor performer or not a team player? Are you uncomfortable staying away from certain issues or projects because you fear missing out on something or aren't sure the work will be done right without you? Most executives we've encountered answer yes to one if not several of those questions.

Efficient collaborators remember that saying yes to something always means saying no to—or participating less fully in—something else. They remind themselves that small wins (an empty in-box, a perfectly worded report, a single client call) are not always important ones. They think carefully about their areas of expertise and determine when they do, or don't, have value to add. They stop seeing themselves as indispensable and shift the source of their self-worth so that it comes from not just showcasing their own capabilities but also stepping away to let others develop theirs and gain visibility.

As one executive told us, "I have come to the realization that if people really need me, they will find me. I am probably skipping 30% of my meetings now, and work seems to be getting done just fine."

When Mike found himself at a breaking point with his twin projects, he realized how much of his self-worth derived from always saying yes to—and then achieving—the goals suggested to him. "It took falling down and a patient spouse to really see this pattern," he says. He decided that he needed to set clear priorities in both his career and his personal life. "Then saying no was not about my not coming through but about maintaining focus on what mattered."

Ellen, too, realized that her self-image as a helper—constantly looking for opportunities to contribute and never declining a request—had become problematic. "The difficult part is recognizing this tendency in the moment and working hard not to jump in," she acknowledges. "But I told my team how important this was and also asked a few people to be 'truth tellers' who caution me when they see it happening."

Eliminating the Unnecessary

Next you'll need to restructure your role, schedule, and network to avoid the triggers you've identified and reduce or eliminate unnecessary collaboration. Rather than thinking things will get better on their own, living reactively, and falling into patterns dictated by other people's objectives, efficient collaborators play offense on collaborative overload. They clarify their "north star" objectives—the strengths they want to employ in their work and the values they want to embody, in the context of their organization's priorities—and then streamline their working lives in a way that buffers them against nonaligned requests.

Start by reviewing your calendar and e-mail communications on a regular basis, using a tool such as Microsoft's MyAnalytics or Cisco's "human network intelligence" platform. Look back four or five months to identify recurring group activities, meetings, or exchanges that aren't core to your success and could be declined or offered to others as a developmental opportunity. Consider decisions you're being pulled into unnecessarily and how processes or teams might be changed so that you needn't be involved. Recognize when you're being sought out for information or expertise in areas no longer central to your role or ambitions and figure out whether you could share your knowledge more widely on your company's intranet or if another go-to person might derive greater benefit from that collaboration.

At the same time, work to reset colleagues' expectations about the level and timeliness of your engagement. Clarify, for example, that not responding to a group e-mail or opting out of a meeting does not mean you lack interest or appreciation. Talk about your key priorities so that everyone knows what you need (and want) to spend the most time on. Ask colleagues about their interests and ambitions so that you can identify opportunities to distribute or delegate work. A key inflection point for all the executives we've counseled has been when they start seeing requests for collaboration as ways to activate and engage those in their networks rather than as adding to their own to-do lists.

Finally, block out time for reflective work and seek collaboration with those who can help you move toward your north star objectives. Mike focused on building capabilities in the business unit he directed. Instead of jumping at unrelated projects for political exposure, he began to differentiate himself through expertise and his team's contribution. Ellen's strategy was to create exceptionally clear boundaries: "I am there 8 a.m. to 6 p.m., and people know I give 100% then. But after that I don't let myself get drawn into unnecessary e-mail, calls, or late-night work just to help out."

Another leader described the shift like this: "Playing defense sucks. You are always reactive and living in fear. The only way to escape it is to get clarity on who you are and what you want to do and start forging a path and network that enable you to get there."

Keeping It Productive

Once you've taken stock of your collaborative workload, it's time to enhance the value of the collaboration you've chosen to participate in. Our research suggests that poorly run meetings are the biggest time sink in organizations. Even if you don't control the ones you attend, you can make them more productive by, for example, asking the leader to circulate an agenda or a pre-read before the gathering and a short e-mail on agreements, commitments, and next steps afterward. You can also limit your involvement by explaining that you have a hard stop (real or constructed) so that you're not stuck when others run overtime, and asking to attend only those portions for which you are needed or agreeing to half the time a colleague or employee requests. It's crucial to establish norms early on in any relationship or group. If you wait, problems will become harder to address.

You can also institute or encourage new norms for e-mails by addressing format (for example, observing a maximum length and choosing an outline structure with bullets, as opposed to full-text paragraphs), the use of "cc" and "reply all," and appropriate response times for various types of requests. Consider virtual collaboration tools (such as Google Docs), which offer a better medium for work that is exploratory (defining a problem space or brainstorming solutions) or integrative (when people with varying expertise, perspectives, or work assignments need to produce a joint solution). The key is to ensure that you're using the right tools at the right time and not worsening collaborative demands. You should also learn to recognize when a conversation has become too complicated or contentious for e-mail or chat and switch to a more efficient phone call or face-to-face meeting.

For one-on-one interactions, always consider whether you are consuming your counterpart's time efficiently. Ask yourself, "Am I clear on what I want to accomplish from a meeting or a conversation?" And invite others to be equally disciplined by asking early on, "So that I use your time well, would you quickly let me know what you hope we can accomplish together?"

When it comes to building your network, focus on the quality of the relationships, not the number of connections. We repeatedly found that efficient collaborators draw people to collaborative work by conferring status, envisioning joint success, diffusing ownership, and generating a sense of purpose and energy around an outcome. By creating "pull"—rather than simply pushing their agenda—they get greater and more-aligned participation and build trust so that people don't feel the need to seek excessive input or approval.

Ellen, for example, decided to engage stakeholders in collaborative work early to save time later in the process. "I used to dot every *i* and cross every *t* before approaching others," she says. "But I've learned that if I get a plan partially developed and then bring in my team, my boss, even my clients, they get invested and help me spot flaws, and I avoid tons of downstream work to fix things or convince people." Another leader we know schedules one-on-ones with direct reports to discuss priorities, values, and personal aspirations, enhancing their ability to work together efficiently as a team in the future. "There are so many ways people can misinterpret actions and then cause a lot of churn later," he says. "If I spend the time to give them a sense of where I'm coming from, it saves all sorts of time in unnecessary collaborations."

The recent explosion in the volume and diversity of collaborative demands is a reality that's here to stay. Unfortunately, the invisible nature of these demands means that few organizations are managing collaborative activity strategically. So it falls to you, the individual, to fight overload and reclaim your collaborative time.

Originally published in July–August 2018. Reprint R1804L

Emotional Agility

by Susan David and Christina Congleton

SIXTEEN THOUSAND—that's how many words we speak, on average, each day. So imagine how many unspoken ones course through our minds. Most of them are not facts but evaluations and judgments entwined with emotions—some positive and helpful (*I've worked hard and I can ace this presentation; This issue is worth speaking up about; The new VP seems approachable*), others negative and less so (*He's purposely ignoring me; I'm going to make a fool of myself; I'm a fake*).

The prevailing wisdom says that difficult thoughts and feelings have no place at the office: Executives, and particularly leaders, should be either stoic or cheerful; they must project confidence and damp down any negativity bubbling up inside them. But that goes against basic biology. All healthy human beings have an inner stream of thoughts and feelings that include criticism, doubt, and fear. That's just our minds doing the job they were designed to do: trying to anticipate and solve problems and avoid potential pitfalls.

In our people-strategy consulting practice advising companies around the world, we see leaders stumble not because they *have* undesirable thoughts and feelings—that's inevitable—but because they get *hooked* by them, like fish caught on a line. This happens in one of two ways. They buy into the thoughts, treating them like facts (*It was the same in my last job . . . I've been a failure my whole career*), and avoid situations that evoke them (*I'm not going to take *on that new challenge).* Or, usually at the behest of their supporters, they challenge the existence of the thoughts and try to rationalize them away (*I shouldn't have thoughts like this . . . I know I'm not a total failure*), and perhaps force themselves into similar situations, even when those go against their core values and goals (*Take on that new assignment—you've got to get over this*). In either case, they are paying too much attention to their internal chatter and allowing it to sap important cognitive resources that could be put to better use.

This is a common problem, often perpetuated by popular self-management strategies. We regularly see executives with recurring emotional challenges at work—anxiety about priorities, jealousy of others' success, fear of rejection, distress over perceived slights—who have devised techniques to "fix" them: positive affirmations, prioritized to-do lists, immersion in certain tasks. But when we ask how long the challenges have persisted, the answer might be 10 years, 20 years, or since childhood.

Clearly, those techniques don't work—in fact, ample research shows that attempting to minimize or ignore thoughts and emotions serves only to amplify them. In a famous study led by the late Daniel Wegner, a Harvard professor, participants who were told to avoid thinking about white bears had trouble doing so; later, when the ban was lifted, they thought about white bears much more than the control group did. Anyone who has dreamed of chocolate cake and French fries while following a strict diet understands this phenomenon.

Effective leaders don't buy into *or* try to suppress their inner experiences. Instead they approach them in a mindful, values-driven, and productive way—developing what we call *emotional agility*. In our complex, fast-changing knowledge economy, this ability to manage one's thoughts and feelings is essential to business success. Numerous studies, from the University of London professor Frank Bond and others, show that emotional agility can help people alleviate stress, reduce errors, become more innovative, and improve job performance.

Idea in Brief

The prevailing wisdom says that negative thoughts and feelings have no place at the office. But that goes against basic biology. All healthy human beings have an inner stream of thoughts and feelings that include criticism, doubt, and fear. David and Congleton have worked with leaders in various industries to build a critical skill they call emotional agility, which enables people to approach their inner experiences in a mindful, values-driven, and productive way rather than buying into or trying to suppress them. The authors offer four practices (adapted from Acceptance and Commitment Therapy, or ACT) designed to help readers do the same:

- **Recognize your patterns.** You have to realize that you're stuck before you can initiate change.

- **Label your thoughts and emotions.** Labeling allows you to see them as transient sources of data that may or may not prove helpful.

- **Accept them.** Respond to your ideas and emotions with an open attitude, paying attention and letting yourself experience them. They may be signaling that something important is at stake.

- **Act on your values.** Is your response going to serve your organization in the long term and take you toward being the leader you most want to be?

We've worked with leaders in various industries to build this critical skill, and here we offer four practices—adapted from Acceptance and Commitment Therapy (ACT), originally developed by the University of Nevada psychologist Steven C. Hayes—that are designed to help you do the same: Recognize your patterns; label your thoughts and emotions; accept them; and act on your values.

Fish on a Line

Let's start with two case studies. Cynthia is a senior corporate lawyer with two young children. She used to feel intense guilt about missed opportunities—both at the office, where her peers worked 80 hours a week while she worked 50, and at home, where she was often too

What Are Your Values?

THIS LIST IS DRAWN from the Personal Values Card Sort (2001), developed by W. R. Miller, J. C'de Baca, D. B. Matthews, and P. L. Wilbourne, of the University of New Mexico. You can use it to quickly identify the values you hold that might inform a challenging situation at work. When you next make a decision, ask yourself whether it is consistent with these values.

Accuracy	Friendship	Passion
Achievement	Fun	Popularity
Adventure	Generosity	Power
Authority	Genuineness	Purpose
Autonomy	Growth	Rationality
Caring	Health	Realism
Challenge	Helpfulness	Responsibility
Change	Honesty	Risk
Comfort	Humility	Safety
Compassion	Humor	Self-knowledge
Contribution	Justice	Service
Cooperation	Knowledge	Simplicity
Courtesy	Leisure	Stability
Creativity	Mastery	Tolerance
Dependability	Moderation	Tradition
Duty	Nonconformity	Wealth
Family	Openness	
Forgiveness	Order	

distracted or tired to fully engage with her husband and children. One nagging voice in her head told her she'd have to be a better employee or risk career failure; another told her to be a better mother or risk neglecting her family. Cynthia wished that at least one of the voices would shut up. But neither would, and in response she failed to put up her hand for exciting new prospects at the office and compulsively checked messages on her phone during family dinners.

Jeffrey, a rising-star executive at a leading consumer goods company, had a different problem. Intelligent, talented, and ambitious, he was often angry—at bosses who disregarded his views, subordinates who didn't follow orders, or colleagues who didn't pull their weight. He had lost his temper several times at work and been warned to get it under control. But when he tried, he felt that he was shutting off a core part of his personality, and he became even angrier and more upset.

These smart, successful leaders were hooked by their negative thoughts and emotions. Cynthia was absorbed by guilt; Jeffrey was exploding with anger. Cynthia told the voices to go away; Jeffrey bottled his frustration. Both were trying to avoid the discomfort they felt. They were being controlled by their inner experience, attempting to control it, or switching between the two.

Getting Unhooked

Fortunately, both Cynthia and Jeffrey realized that they couldn't go on—at least not successfully and happily—without more-effective inner strategies. We coached them to adopt the four practices.

Recognize your patterns

The first step in developing emotional agility is to notice when you've been hooked by your thoughts and feelings. That's hard to do, but there are certain telltale signs. One is that your thinking becomes rigid and repetitive. For example, Cynthia began to see that her self-recriminations played like a broken record, repeating the same messages over and over again. Another is that the story your mind is telling seems old, like a rerun of some past experience. Jeffrey noticed that his attitude toward certain colleagues (*He's incompetent; There's no way I'm letting anyone speak to me like that*) was quite familiar. In fact, he had experienced something similar in his previous job—and in the one before that. The source of trouble was not just Jeffrey's environment but his own patterns of thought and feeling. You have to realize that you're stuck before you can initiate change.

Label your thoughts and emotions

When you're hooked, the attention you give your thoughts and feelings crowds your mind; there's no room to examine them. One strategy that may help you consider your situation more objectively is the simple act of labeling. Just as you call a spade a spade, call a thought a thought and an emotion an emotion. *I'm not doing enough at work or at home* becomes *I'm having the thought that I'm not doing enough at work or at home.* Similarly, *My coworker is wrong—he makes me so angry* becomes *I'm having the thought that my coworker is wrong, and I'm feeling anger.* Labeling allows you to see your thoughts and feelings for what they are: transient sources of data that may or may not prove helpful. Humans are psychologically able to take this helicopter view of private experiences, and mounting scientific evidence shows that simple, straightforward mindfulness practice like this not only improves behavior and well-being but also promotes beneficial biological changes in the brain and at the cellular level. As Cynthia started to slow down and label her thoughts, the criticisms that had once pressed in on her like a dense fog became more like clouds passing through a blue sky.

Accept them

The opposite of control is acceptance—not acting on every thought or resigning yourself to negativity but responding to your ideas and emotions with an open attitude, paying attention to them and letting yourself experience them. Take 10 deep breaths and notice what's happening in the moment. This can bring relief, but it won't necessarily make you feel good. In fact, you may realize just how upset you really are. The important thing is to show yourself (and others) some compassion and examine the reality of the situation. What's going on—both internally and externally? When Jeffrey acknowledged and made room for his feelings of frustration and anger rather than rejecting them, quashing them, or taking them out on others, he began to notice their energetic quality. They were a signal that something important was at stake and that he needed to take productive action. Instead of yelling at people, he could make a clear request of a colleague or move swiftly on a pressing issue. The more Jeffrey accepted his anger and brought his curiosity to it, the more it seemed to support rather than undermine his leadership.

Evaluate your emotional agility

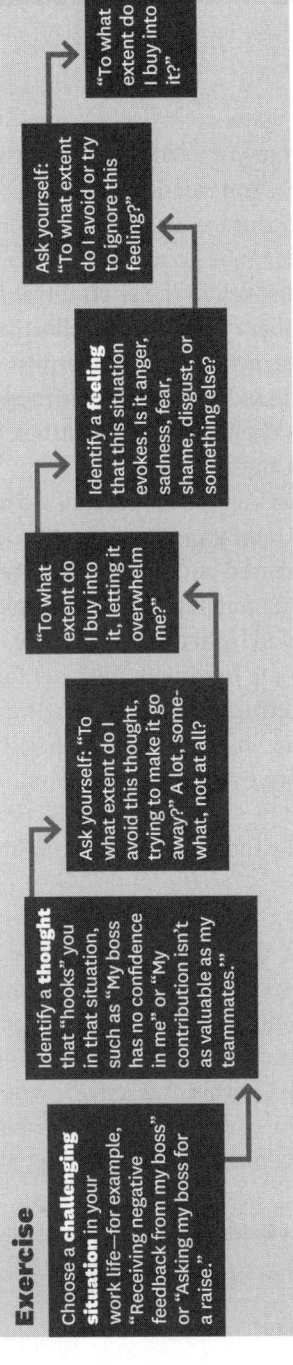

Exercise

Choose a **challenging situation** in your work life—for example, "Receiving negative feedback from my boss" or "Asking my boss for a raise."

Identify a **thought** that "hooks" you in that situation, such as "My boss has no confidence in me" or "My contribution isn't as valuable as my teammates.'"

Ask yourself: "To what extent do I avoid this thought, trying to make it go away?" A lot, somewhat, not at all?

"To what extent do I buy into it, letting it overwhelm me?"

Identify a **feeling** that this situation evokes. Is it anger, sadness, fear, shame, disgust, or something else?

Ask yourself: "To what extent do I avoid or try to ignore this feeling?"

"To what extent do I buy into it?"

Advice

If you primarily **avoid** your thoughts and feelings, try to acknowledge them instead. Notice thoughts as they arise and check your emotional state several times a day so that you can identify the useful information your mind is sending you.

If you primarily **buy into** your thoughts and feelings, find your ground. Take 10 deep breaths, notice your environment, and label—rather than being swept up in—them.

If you **alternate**, learn your patterns. Pay attention to which thoughts and feelings you avoid and which you buy into so that you can respond with one of the strategies we describe.

The next step is to take action that aligns with your **values.** (For examples, see the sidebar "What Are Your Values?") Identify which ones you want to apply in the context of the challenging situation you've described.

Act on your values

When you unhook yourself from your difficult thoughts and emotions, you expand your choices. You can decide to act in a way that aligns with your values. We encourage leaders to focus on the concept of *workability*: Is your response going to serve you and your organization in the long term as well as the short term? Will it help you steer others in a direction that furthers your collective purpose? Are you taking a step toward being the leader you most want to be and living the life you most want to live? The mind's thought stream flows endlessly, and emotions change like the weather, but values can be called on at any time, in any situation.

When Cynthia considered her values, she recognized how deeply committed she was to both her family and her work; she loved being with her children, but she also cared passionately about the pursuit of justice. Unhooked from her distracting and discouraging feelings of guilt, she resolved to be guided by her principles. She recognized how important it was to get home for dinner with her family every evening and to resist work interruptions during that time. But she also undertook to make a number of important business trips, some of which coincided with school events that she would have preferred to attend. Confident that her values, not solely her emotions, were guiding her, Cynthia finally found peace and fulfillment.

It's impossible to block out difficult thoughts and emotions. Effective leaders are mindful of their inner experiences but not caught in them. They know how to free up their internal resources and commit to actions that align with their values. Developing emotional agility is no quick fix—even those who, like Cynthia and Jeffrey, regularly practice the steps we've outlined here will often find themselves hooked. But over time, leaders who become increasingly adept at it are the ones most likely to thrive.

Originally published in November 2013. Reprint R1311L

How to Tackle Your Toughest Decisions

by Joseph L. Badaracco

EVERY MANAGER makes tough calls—it comes with the job. And the toughest calls come in the gray areas—situations where you and your team have worked hard to gather the facts and done the best analysis you can, but you still don't know what to do. It's easy to become paralyzed in the face of such challenges. Yet as a leader, you have to make a decision and move forward. Your judgment becomes critical.

Judgment is hard to define. It is a fusion of your thinking, feelings, experience, imagination, and character. But five practical questions can improve your odds of making sound judgments, even when the data is incomplete or unclear, opinions are divided, and the answers are far from obvious.

Where do these questions come from? Over many centuries and across many cultures, they have emerged as men and women with serious responsibilities have struggled with difficult problems. They express the insights of the most penetrating minds and compassionate spirits of human history. I have relied on them for years, in teaching MBA candidates and counseling executives, and I believe that they can help you, your team, and your organization navigate the grayest of gray areas.

This article explains the five questions and illustrates them with a disguised case study involving a manager who must decide what to do about a persistently underperforming employee who has failed to respond to suggestions for improvement. He deserves a bad review, if not dismissal, but higher-ups at the company want to overlook his failings.

How should the manager approach this situation? Not by following her gut instinct. Not by simply falling into line. Instead, she needs to systematically work through the five questions:

What are the net, net consequences of all my options?

What are my core obligations?

What will work in the world as it is? Who are we?

What can I live with?

To grapple with these questions, you must rely on the best information and expertise available. But in the end you have to answer them for yourself. With gray-area decisions, you can never be certain you've made the right call. But if you follow this process, you'll know that you worked on the problem in the right way—not just as a good manager but as a thoughtful human being.

Net, Net Consequences

The first question asks you to thoroughly and analytically consider every course of action available to you, along with the full, real-world, human consequences of each. Gray-area problems are rarely resolved in a flash of intuitive brilliance from one person; as a very successful CEO told me, "The lonely leader on Olympus is really a bad model." So your job is to put aside your initial assumption about what you *should* do, gather a group of trusted advisers and experts, and ask yourself and them, "What *could* we do? And who will be hurt or helped, short-term and long-term, by each option?"

Don't confuse this with cost-benefit analysis, or focus solely on what you can count or price. Of course, you should get the best data you can and apply the relevant frameworks. But gray-area problems require you to think more broadly, deeply, concretely, imaginatively, and objectively about the full impact of your choices. In the words of the ancient Chinese philosopher Mozi, "It is the business of the

Idea in Brief

The toughest calls managers have to make come in situations when they have worked hard to gather the facts and have done the best analysis they can, but they still don't know what to do. Then judgment—a fusion of thinking, feelings, experience, imagination, and character—becomes critical. Five practical questions can improve your odds of making sound judgments:

- What are the net, net consequences of all my options?

- What are my core obligations?

- What will work in the world as it is?

- Who are we?

- What can I live with?

With gray-area decisions, you can never be certain that you've made the right call. But if you work through these questions, you'll know that you've approached the problem in the right way—not just as a good manager but as a thoughtful human being.

benevolent man to seek to promote what is beneficial to the world and to eliminate what is harmful."

In today's complex, fluid, interdependent world, none of us can predict the future with total accuracy. And it's sometimes hard to think clearly about gray-area issues. What's important is taking the time to open your mind, assemble the right team, and analyze your options through a humanist lens. You might sketch out a rough decision tree, listing all potential moves and all probable outcomes, or designate certain people to act as devil's advocates to find holes in your thinking and prevent you from rushing to conclusions or succumbing to groupthink.

When you make important, difficult decisions, you affect many people's lives and livelihoods. The first question asks you to grapple hard with that reality.

Core Obligations

We all have duties—as parents, children, citizens, employees. Managers also have duties to shareholders and other stakeholders. But the second question gets at something deeper: the duties we have to safeguard and respect the lives, rights, and dignity of our fellow men and women.

All the world's great religions—Islam, Judaism, Hinduism, Christianity—emphasize this obligation. The contemporary ethicist Kwame Anthony Appiah has said, "No local loyalty can ever justify forgetting that each human being has responsibilities to every other."

How can you figure out specifically what these duties oblige you to do in a particular situation? By relying on what philosophers call your "moral imagination." That involves stepping out of your comfort zone, recognizing your biases and blind spots, and putting yourself in the shoes of all key stakeholders, especially the most vulnerable ones. How would you feel in their place? What would you be most concerned about or afraid of? How would you want to be treated? What would you see as fair? What rights would you believe you had? What would you consider to be hateful? You might speak directly to the people who will be affected by your decision, or ask a member of your team to role-play the outsider or victim as persuasively as he or she can.

Again, you must look past economics and your business school training. Yes, managers have a legal duty to serve the corporation—but that's a very broad mandate that includes the well-being of workers, customers, and the community in which they operate. You have serious obligations to everyone simply because you are a human being. When you face a gray-area decision, you have to think—long, hard, and personally—about which of these duties stands at the head of the line.

The World as It Is

The third question pushes you to look at your problem in a clear-eyed, pragmatic way—seeing the world not as you would like it to be but as it is. Ultimately you need a plan that will work—one that will move an individual, a team, a department, or an entire organization through a gray area responsibly and successfully.

The phrase "the world as it is" points toward Niccolò Machiavelli's thinking—a perspective that might seem surprising in an article about making responsible decisions. But his view is important, because it acknowledges that we don't live in a predictable, calm environment populated with virtuous people. The world Machiavelli described is unpredictable, difficult, and shaped by self-interest. Sound plans can turn out badly, and bad plans sometimes work. Much of what happens is simply beyond our control. Leaders rarely have unlimited freedom and resources, so they must often make painful choices. And a great many individuals and groups will pursue their own agendas, skillfully or clumsily, if not persuaded to do otherwise.

That is why, after considering consequences and duties, you need to think about practicalities: Of the possible solutions to your problem, which is most likely to work? Which is most resilient? And how resilient and flexible are you?

To answer those questions, you need to map the force field of power around you: who wants what and how hard and successfully each person can fight for his aims. You must also ready yourself to be agile and even opportunistic—maneuvering around any roadblocks or surprises—and, when the situation calls for it, to play hardball, asserting your authority and reminding others who is the boss.

It's easy to misinterpret the third question as an "out"—an excuse to do what's safe and expedient instead of the right thing. But the question is really about what will work if you bring persistence, dedication, creativity, prudent risk-taking, and political savvy to the task.

Who Are We?

According to an old African adage, "I am because we are." Put differently, our behavior and identities are shaped by the groups in which we work and live. As Aristotle said (and as a vast body of scientific literature has since confirmed), "Man is by nature a social animal." So this question asks you to step back and think about your decision in terms of relationships, values, and norms. What really matters to your team, company, community, culture? How can you act in a way that reflects and expresses those belief systems? If they conflict, which should take precedence?

To answer those questions, you might think about the defining stories of a particular group—the decisions and incidents that everyone cites when explaining the ideals to which you are collectively committed, what you have struggled to achieve, and what outcomes you try hard to avoid. Imagine that you are writing a sentence or a chapter in your company's history. Of all the paths you might choose in this gray area, which would best express what your organization stands for?

This question comes fourth because you shouldn't start with it. Unlike the first three, which require you to take an outsider's perspective on your situation and consider it as objectively as possible, this one addresses you as an insider, at risk for adopting an insular, limited view when you consider norms and values, because we are naturally inclined to take care of our own. So counterbalance that tendency with the thinking prompted by the previous questions.

Living with Your Decision

Good judgment relies on two things: One is the best possible understanding and analysis of the situation. The other involves the values, ideals, vulnerabilities, and experiences of whoever will be making the decision. A seasoned executive once told me, "I wouldn't go ahead with something just because my brain told me it was the right thing to do. I also had to feel it. If I didn't, I had to get my brain and my gut into harmony."

Ultimately you must choose, commit to, act on, and live with the consequences of your choice. So it must also reflect what you really care about as a manager and a human being. After considering outcomes, duties, practicalities, and values, you must decide what matters most and what matters less. This has always been the challenge of taking on any serious responsibilities at work and in life.

How will you figure out what you can live with? End your conversations with others, close the door, mute the electronics, and stop to reflect. Imagine yourself explaining your decision to a close friend or a mentor—someone you trust and respect deeply. Would you feel comfortable? How would that person react? It may also be helpful to write down your decision and your reasons for it: Writing forces clearer thinking and serves as a form of personal commitment.

In Practice

Now let's turn to our case study. Becky Friedman was the 27-year-old manager of a 14-person technology group responsible for clothing sales at an online retailer. One of her team members, Terry Fletcher, a man 15 years her senior with a longer tenure at the company, wasn't doing his part. Although his previous boss had routinely given him scores of 3.5 on their five-point performance scale, Friedman didn't believe his work merited that; and whenever she presented him with opportunities to develop his skills and ramp up his contributions, he failed to follow through. So she wanted to drop his rating to 2.5 and put him on a performance improvement plan (PIP), on a path to dismissal. Soon, however, two of the company's vice presidents, good friends of Fletcher's, caught wind of her plans and paid her a visit. They asked whether she was sure about what she was doing and suggested that the real problem might be her management.

Suddenly the situation was no longer black-and-white. Friedman had entered a gray area and felt stuck. To find a way out, she turned to the five questions. She considered her options—stick to her plan, abandon it, or find a middle ground—and their consequences. She reminded herself of her basic duties to her fellow human beings, including Fletcher, her team, and the VPs. She evaluated the practical realities of her organization. She weighed the defining norms and values of her various social groups. And she thought carefully about her own abiding sense of what really matters in life.

She suspected that if she pushed forward and gave Fletcher the rating he deserved, she and her team would suffer retribution: The VPs could withhold resources or even force her out of the company. She also worried about Fletcher, who seemed off-balance and appeared to have few things going well in his life. How would a poor review and a possible job loss affect him, not just financially but also psychologically? If Friedman chose option B, however, she would still have a deadweight on her team, which might prevent the group from achieving its ambitious goals and demoralize its most talented and diligent members. The VPs might also take her capitulation as a sign of weakness, which could keep her, a relative newcomer, from moving up in the leadership ranks.

Middle-ground options, such as presenting Fletcher with further development opportunities or giving him another warning, seemed more promising but carried their own risks: Would they be effective in changing his behavior? Would they still result in backlash from the VPs? Friedman also thought about what she, her team, and her organization cared about most. As a woman in computer science, she knew what it was like to be marginalized, as Fletcher was among the whiz kids in her department, and she felt compelled to help him. At the same time, her group prided itself on exceptionally professional performance, and her company, although young, had always claimed and generally proved to be a meritocracy with high standards and a sharp focus on customer needs.

After much deliberation, Friedman decided to try a counseling session with Fletcher. She opened by telling him that she had decided to give him a 2.5, but that she wouldn't put him on a PIP because it would be too demeaning. She then asked him to consider the department's recent hires—all of whom had strong technical skills—and honestly evaluate whether he would be happy or successful working alongside them. She concluded by suggesting that he spend the next several months continuing to do his job while also looking for another one. She was surprised and relieved when his immediate anger over the bad rating subsided and he agreed to consider her plan; in fact, he had already been toying with the idea of leaving. He spent the next several weeks looking for other positions, inside the company and elsewhere, and soon joined another company. Friedman, meanwhile, continued to thrive. She had, of course, been lucky; there was no guarantee that Fletcher would respond so positively to her feedback. But she'd put herself in a good position by getting the process right, and she'd been prepared to try other, equally thought-through tactics if the first didn't work.

When you face a gray-area problem, be sure to systematically answer *all five* of the questions, just as Becky Friedman did. Don't simply pick your favorite. Each question is an important voice in the centuries-long conversation about what counts as a sound decision regarding a hard problem with high stakes for other people.

Leadership can be a heavy burden. It is also a compelling, crucial challenge. In gray areas, your job isn't *finding* solutions; it's *creating* them, relying on your judgment. As an executive I greatly respect once told me, "We really want someone or some rule to tell us what to do. But sometimes there isn't one, and *you* have to decide what the most relevant rules or principles are in this particular case. You can't escape that responsibility."

Originally published in September 2016. Reprint R1609J

How Dual-Career Couples Make It Work

by Jennifer Petriglieri

CAMILLE AND PIERRE MET in their early forties after each one's marriage had ended. Both were deeply committed to their careers and to their new relationship. Camille, an accountant, had felt pressured by her ex-husband to slow her progress toward partnership at her firm. Pierre, a production manager at an automotive company, was embroiled in a bitter divorce from his wife, who had given up her career to accommodate the geographic moves that his required. (As with the other couples I've profiled in this article, these aren't their real names.) Bruised by their past experiences, they agreed to place their careers on an equal footing. Initially things went smoothly, but two years in, Camille began to feel trapped on a professional path that she realized she had chosen because "that was what the smart kids did."

Mindful of their pact, Pierre calmly listened to her doubts and encouraged her to explore alternatives. But as the months wore on, he began to feel weighed down as he juggled providing emotional support to Camille, navigating their complex family logistics (both had children from their former marriages), and succeeding in his demanding job. When he began to question his own career direction, he wondered how the two of them could manage to change course. They couldn't afford to take time out from work, nor could they take much time to reflect and keep their family and relationship afloat. Frustrated and exhausted, both wondered how they could continue to find meaning and fulfillment in their lives.

Dual-earner couples are on the rise. According to Pew Research, in 63% of couples with children in the United States, for example, both partners work (this figure is slightly higher in the EU). Many of these are *dual-career couples:* Both partners are highly educated, work full-time in demanding professional or managerial jobs, and see themselves on an upward path in their roles. For these couples, as for Pierre and Camille, work is a primary source of identity and a primary channel for ambition. Evidence is mounting from sociological research that when both partners dedicate themselves to work and to home life, they reap benefits such as increased economic freedom, a more satisfying relationship, and a lower-than-average chance of divorce.

Because their working lives and personal lives are deeply intertwined, however, dual-career couples face unique challenges. How do they decide whose job to relocate for, when it's OK for one partner to make a risky career change, or who will leave work early to pick up a sick child from school? How can they give family commitments—and each other—their full attention while both of them are working in demanding roles? And when one of them wants to undertake a professional reinvention, what does that mean for the other? They must work out these questions together, in a way that lets both thrive in love and work. If they don't, regrets and imbalances quickly build up, threatening to hinder their careers, dissolve their relationship, or both.

Many of these challenges are well recognized, and I've previously written in HBR about how companies can adapt their talent strategies to account for some of them ("Talent Management and the Dual-Career Couple," May–June 2018). But for the couples themselves, little guidance is available. Most advice treats major career decisions as if one is flying solo, without a partner, children, or aging parents to consider. When it's for couples, it focuses on their relationship, not how that intersects with their professional dreams, or it addresses how to balance particular trade-offs, such as careers ver-

Idea in Brief

The Problem

When both members of a couple have demanding careers, their work and personal lives are deeply intertwined—and often at odds.

The Transitions

Dual-career couples tend to go through three phases of being particularly vulnerable: when they first learn to work together as a couple; when they experience a midlife reinvention; and in the final stages of their working lives.

The Solution

Couples who communicate at each transition about values, boundaries, and fears have a good chance of being fulfilled both in their relationships and in their careers.

sus family, or how to prioritize partners' work travel. What couples need is a more comprehensive approach for managing the moments when commitments and aspirations clash.

My personal experience in a dual-career couple, and my realization that little systematic academic research had been done in this area, prompted a six-year investigation into the lives of more than 100 dual-career couples, resulting in my book, *Couples That Work*. The people I studied come from around the world, range in age from mid-twenties to mid-sixties, and represent a range of professions, from corporate executive to entrepreneur to worker in the non-profit sector. (See the sidebar "About the Research.") My research revealed that dual-career couples overcome their challenges by directly addressing deeper psychological and social forces—such as struggles for power and control; personal hopes, fears, and losses; and assumptions and cultural expectations about the roles partners should play in each other's lives and what it means to have a good relationship or career.

I also discovered that three transition points typically occur during dual-career couples' working and love lives, when those forces are particularly strong. It is during these transitions, I found, that some couples craft a way to thrive in love and work, while others are plagued by conflict and regret. By understanding each transition and knowing what questions to ask each other and what traps

About the Research

I STUDIED 113 DUAL-CAREER COUPLES. They ranged in age from 26 to 63, with an even distribution among age groups. The majority of couples—76—were in their first significant partnership. Participants in the study came from 32 countries on four continents, and their ethnic and religious backgrounds reflected this diversity. At the time of the study, roughly 35% resided in North America, 40% in Europe, and 25% in the rest of the world. In 68 of the couples at least one partner had children. Eleven of the couples identified as gay, and the rest as straight. Just under 60% of the participants were pursuing careers in the corporate world. The others were spread roughly equally among the professions (such as medicine, law, and academia), entrepreneurship, government, and the nonprofit sector.

I interviewed the members of each couple separately, asking them about the development of their relationships, their career paths, their interactions as a couple, and their family and friend networks.

to avoid, dual-career couples can emerge stronger, fulfilled in their relationships and in their careers.

Transition 1: Working as a Couple

When Jamal and Emily met, in their late twenties, trade-offs were the last thing on their minds. They were full of energy, optimistic, and determined to live life to the fullest. Jamal, a project manager in a civil engineering firm, traveled extensively for work and was given increasingly complex projects to lead, while Emily, who worked at a clothing company, had just been promoted to her first management role. They saw each other mostly on weekends, which they often spent on wilderness hiking adventures. They married 18 months after their first date.

Then, in the space of three months, their world changed dramatically. While Emily was pregnant with their first child, Jamal's boss asked him to run a critical infrastructure project in Mexico. Jamal agreed to spend three weeks out of every month in Mexico City; designating some of his pay raise to extra child care would allow Emily to keep working in Houston, where they lived. But when their daughter, Aisha, was born two weeks early, Jamal was stuck in the

Mexico City airport waiting for a flight home. Soon Emily, who was single-handedly managing Aisha, her job, and their home, discovered that the additional child care wasn't enough; she felt overburdened and unappreciated. Jamal was exhausted by the relentless travel and the stress of the giant new project; he felt isolated, incompetent, and guilty.

After many arguments, they settled on what they hoped was a practical solution: Because Jamal earned more, Emily took a smaller project role that she could manage remotely, and she and Aisha joined him in Mexico. But Emily felt disconnected from her company's head office and was passed over for a promotion, and eventually she grew resentful of the arrangement. By the time Jamal's boss began talking about his next assignment, their fighting had become intense.

The first transition that dual-career couples must navigate often comes as a response to the first major life event they face together—typically a big career opportunity, the arrival of a child, or the merger of families from previous relationships. To adapt, the partners must negotiate how to prioritize their careers and divide family commitments. Doing so in a way that lets them both thrive requires an underlying shift: They must move from having parallel, independent careers and lives to having interdependent ones.

My research shows two common traps for couples negotiating their way through their first transition:

Concentrating exclusively on the practical
In the first transition in particular, couples often look for logistical solutions to their challenges, as Jamal and Emily did when they arranged for extra child care and negotiated how many weekends Jamal would be home. This focus is understandable—such problems are tangible, and the underlying psychological and social tensions are murky and anxiety provoking—but it prolongs the struggle, because those tensions remain unresolved.

Instead of simply negotiating over calendars and to-do lists, couples must understand, share, and discuss the emotions, values, and fears underlying their decisions. Talking about feelings as well as practicalities can help them mitigate and manage them.

A Guide to Couple Contracting

DRAWING ON MY RESEARCH, I've developed a systematic tool to help dual-career couples who are facing any of the three transitions described in this article. I call it *couple contracting*, because to shape their joint path, partners must address three areas—values, boundaries, and fears—and find common ground in each. Values define the direction of your path, boundaries set its borders, and fears reveal the potential cliffs to avoid on either side. Sharing a clear view in these three domains will make it easier to negotiate and overcome the challenges you encounter together.

First, take some time on your own to write down your thoughts about each of the three areas. Then share your reflections with each other. Listen to and acknowledge each other's responses, resisting any temptation to diminish or discount your partner's fears. Next, note where you have common ground and where your values and boundaries diverge. No couple has perfect overlap in those two areas, but if they are too divergent, negotiate a middle ground. If, for example, one of you could tolerate living apart for a period but the other could not, you'll need to shape a boundary that works for both of you.

Values

When our choices and actions align with our values, we feel content; when they don't, we feel stressed and unhappy. Openly discussing your values will make it easier to make choices that align with them. For example, if you and your partner know you both greatly value family time, you'll be clear that neither of you should take a job requiring 70-hour workweeks.

Questions to ask each other

What makes you happy and proud? What gives you satisfaction? What makes for a good life?

Basing decisions primarily on money

Many couples focus on economic gain as they decide where to live, whose career to prioritize, and who will do the majority of the child care. But as sensible (and sometimes unavoidable) as this is, it often means that their decisions end up at odds with their other values and desires.

Few people live for financial gain alone. In their careers they are also motivated by continual learning and being given greater

Boundaries

Setting clear boundaries together allows you to make big decisions more easily. Consider three types of boundaries: place, time, and presence.

Questions to ask each other

Are there places where you'd love to work and live at some point in your life? Are there places you'd prefer to avoid? Understanding that we may sometimes have to put in more hours than we'd like, how much work is too much? How would you feel about our taking jobs in different cities and living apart for a period? For how long? How much work travel is too much, and how will we juggle travel between us?

Fears

Monitoring each other's fears can help you spot trouble and take preventive action before your relationship enters dangerous territory. Many fears are endemic to relationships and careers: You may worry that your partner's family will encroach on your relationship, that over time the two of you will grow apart, that your partner will have an affair, that you will have to sacrifice your career for your partner's, or that you may not be able to have children. But sharing these fears allows you to build greater empathy and support. If you know that your partner is worried about the role of your parents in your lives, for example, you are more likely to manage the boundary between them and your partnership sensitively. Likewise, if you are interested in a risky career transition but worried that financial commitments would prevent it, you might agree to cut back on family spending in order to build a buffer.

Questions to ask each other

What are your concerns for the future? What's your biggest fear about how our relationship and careers interact? What do you dread might happen in our lives?

---

responsibilities. Outside work, they want to spend time with their children and pursue personal interests. Couples may be attracted to a location because of proximity to extended family, the quality of life it affords, or their ability to build a strong community. Basing the decision to move to Mexico on Jamal's higher salary meant that he and Emily ignored their other interests, feeding their discontent.

Couples who are successful discuss the foundations and the structure of their joint path forward. First, they must come to some agreement on core aspects of their relationship: their values, boundaries, and fears. (See the sidebar "A Guide to Couple Contracting.") Negotiating and finding common ground in these areas helps them navigate difficult decisions because they can agree on criteria in advance. Doing this together is important; couples that make this arrangement work, I found, make choices openly and jointly, rather than implicitly and for each other. The ones I studied who had never addressed their core criteria struggled in later transitions, because those criteria never go away.

Next, couples must discuss how to prioritize their careers and divide family commitments. Striving for 50/50 is not always the best option; neither must one decide to always give the other's career priority.

There are three basic models to consider: (1) In *primary-secondary,* one partner's career takes priority over the other's for the duration of their working lives. The primary person dedicates more time to work and less to the family, and his or her professional commitments (and geographic requirements) usually come before the secondary person's. (2) In *turn taking,* the partners agree to periodically swap the primary and secondary positions. (3) In *double-primary,* they continually juggle two primary careers.

My research shows that couples can feel fulfilled in their careers and relationships whichever model they pursue, as long as it aligns with their values and they openly discuss and explicitly agree on their options. Couples who pursue the third option are often the most successful, although it's arguably the most difficult, precisely because they are forced to address conflicts most frequently.

To work past their deadlock, Emily and Jamal finally discussed what really mattered to them beyond financial success. They identified pursuit of their chosen careers, proximity to nature, and a stable home for Aisha where they could both actively parent her. They admitted their fears of growing apart, and in response agreed to an important restriction: They would live in the same city and would limit work travel to 25% of their time. They agreed to place their geographic boundaries around North America, and Jamal suggested that they both draw circles on a map around the cities where they felt they could make a home and have two careers. Their conversations and mapping exercise eventually brought them to a resolution—and a new start in Atlanta, where they would pursue a double-primary model. Three years later they are progressing in their careers, happy in their family life, and expecting a second child.

Transition 2: Reinventing Themselves

Psychological theory holds that early in life many people follow career and personal paths that conform to the expectations of their parents, friends, peers, and society, whereas in their middle years many feel a pressing need for *individuation,* or breaking free of those expectations to become authors of their own lives. This tends to happen in people's forties, regardless of their relationship status, and is part of a process colloquially known as the midlife crisis.

We tend to think of a midlife crisis mostly in personal terms (a husband leaves his wife, for example, and buys a sports car), but in dual-career couples, the intense focus on professional success means that the partners' job tracks come under scrutiny as well. This combined personal and professional crisis forms the basis of the second transition. Camille and Pierre, whose story began this article, were in the midst of it.

As each partner wrestles with self-redefinition, the two often bump up against long-settled arrangements they have made and the identities, relationship, and careers they have crafted together. Some of those arrangements—whose career takes precedence, for example—may need to be reconsidered to allow one partner to quit a job and explore alternatives. It may be painful to question the choices they made together during the previous transition and have since built their lives around. This can be threatening to a relationship; it's not uncommon for one partner to interpret the other's desire to rethink past career choices as an inclination to rethink the relationship as well, or even to potentially end it. Couples who handle this transition well find ways to connect with and support each other through what can feel like a very solitary process.

The second transition often begins—as it did for Camille and Pierre—when one partner reexamines a career or life path. That person must reflect on questions such as: What led me to this impasse? Why did I make the choices I made? Who am I? What do I desire from life? Whom do I want to become? He or she should also take time to explore alternative paths, through networking events, job shadowing, secondments, volunteer work, and so forth. Such individual reflection and exploration can lead couples to the first trap of the second transition:

Mistrust and defensiveness
Living with a partner who is absorbed in exploring new paths can feel threatening. Painful questions surface: Why is my partner not satisfied? Is this a career problem or a relationship problem? Am I to blame? Why does he or she need new people? Am I no longer enough? These doubts can lead to mistrust and defensiveness, which may push the exploring partner to withdraw further from the relationship, making the other even more mistrustful and defensive, until eventually the relationship itself becomes an obstacle to individuation, rather than a space for it.

In such a situation, people should first be open about their concerns and let their partners reassure them that the angst is not about them or the relationship. Next, they should adopt what literary critics call *suspension of disbelief*—that is, faith that the things they have doubts about will unfold in interesting ways and are worth paying attention to. This attitude will both enrich their own lives and make their partners' exploration easier.

Finally, they should understand their role as supporters. Psychologists call this role in a relationship the *secure base* and see it as vital to the other partner's growth. Originally identified and described by the psychologist John Bowlby, the secure base allows us to stretch ourselves by stepping outside our comfort zone while someone by our side soothes our anxieties about doing so. Without overly interfering, supporters should encourage their partners' exploration and reflection, even if it means moving away from the comfortable relationship they've already established.

Being a secure base for a partner presents its own trap, however:

Asymmetric support

In some couples one partner consistently supports the other without receiving support in return. That's what happened to Camille and Pierre. Pierre's experience in his former marriage, in which his wife gave up her career for his, made him determined to support Camille, and he initially stepped up to be a secure base for her. Their lives were so packed, however, that Camille had trouble finding the energy to return the favor. The result was that her exploration and reflection became an impediment to Pierre's, creating a developmental and relationship deadlock. It is important to remember that acting as a secure base does not mean annihilating your own wishes, atoning for past selfishness, or being perfect. You can be a wonderful supporter for your partner while requesting support in return and taking time for yourself. In fact, that will most likely make you a far better (and less resentful) supporter.

In my research I found that couples who make it through their second transition are those in which the partners encourage each other to do this work—even if it means that one of them is exploring and providing support at the same time.

Once the exploring partner has had a chance to determine what he or she wants in a career, a life, or a relationship, the next step is to make it happen—as a couple. Couples need to renegotiate the roles they play in each other's lives. Take Matthew and James, another pair I spoke with, who had risen through the professional ranks in their 18 years together. When Matthew realized that he wanted to get off what he called the success train—on which he felt like a mere passenger—both he and James had to let go of their identity as a power couple and revisit the career-prioritization agreement they had forged during their first transition. Initially Matthew was reluctant to talk to James about his doubts, because he questioned whether James would still love him if he changed direction. When they started discussing this, however, they realized that their identity as a power couple had trapped them in a dynamic in which both needed to succeed but neither could outshine the other.

Acknowledging and renegotiating this unspoken arrangement allowed James to shoot for his first senior executive position and Matthew to transition into the nonprofit sector. The time and care they took to answer their existential questions and renegotiate the roles they played in each other's lives set them up for a renewed period of growth in their careers and in their relationship.

Transition 3: Loss and Opportunity

Attending her mother's funeral was one of the most difficult experiences of Norah's life. It was the culmination of two years of immense change for her and her husband, Jeremy, who were in their late fifties. The change began when their fathers unexpectedly passed away within five weeks of each other, and they became caregivers for Norah's ailing mother just as their children were leaving the nest and their own careers were in flux.

Jeremy is a digital visual artist. His studio's main projects were ending because a big client was moving on. Though he was sad, he had become confident enough to feel excited about whatever might come next. Norah had been working for the same small agricultural machinery business for 26 years; she had once wanted to change careers but felt that she couldn't do so while Jeremy was relying on her for emotional and logistical support. Now she was being asked to take an early retirement deal. She felt thrown on the scrap heap despite her long commitment to the company. No career, no parents, no children to care for—who was she now? She felt disoriented and adrift.

The third transition is typically triggered by shifting roles later in life, which often create a profound sense of loss. Careers plateau or decline; bodies are no longer what they once were; children, if there are any, leave home. Sometimes one partner's career is going strong while the other's begins to ebb. Having raced through decades of career growth and child-rearing, couples wake up with someone who may have changed since the time they fell in love. They may both feel that way. These changes again raise fundamental questions of identity: Who am I now? Who do I want to be for the rest of my life?

Although loss usually triggers it, the third transition heralds opportunity. Chances for late-in-life reinvention abound, especially in today's world. Life expectancy is rising across the globe, and older couples may have several decades of reasonably good health and freedom from intensive parenting responsibilities. As careers and work become more flexible, especially for those with experience, people can engage in multiple activities more easily than previous generations could—combining advisory or consulting work with board service, for example. Their activities often include giving back to the community, leaving some kind of legacy, mentoring younger generations, rediscovering passions of their youth, or dedicating themselves more to friendships.

Their task in the third transition is to again reinvent themselves—this time in a way that is both grounded in past accomplishments and optimistic about possibilities for the future. They must mourn the old, welcome the new, figure out how the two fit together, and adjust their life path to support who they want to become.

One thing that struck me when I spoke to couples in their third transition is that it's most powerful when partners reinvent themselves together—not just reflecting jointly, as in the other transitions, but actually taking on a new activity or project side by side. When one is curious about a partner's life and work as well as one's own, an immense capacity for mutual revitalization is unlocked. I met many couples who were charting new paths out of this transition that involved a merging of their work—launching a new business together, for example.

The third transition also has its traps:

Unfinished business

For better or for worse, earlier relational patterns, approaches, decisions, and assumptions will influence how a couple's third transition unfolds. I found that the most common challenge in managing this transition was overcoming regret about perceived failures in the way the partners had "worked" as a couple—how they had prioritized their careers, or how each partner had supported the other's development (or not).

To move through the third transition, couples must acknowledge how they got where they are and commit to playing new roles for each other in the future. For example, Norah and Jeremy had become stuck in a pattern in which Norah was Jeremy's supporter. By recognizing this—and both their roles in cementing it—they were able to become more mutually supportive.

Narrow horizons

By the time a couple reaches the third transition, they will probably have suffered their fair share of disappointments and setbacks. They may be tired from years of taking care of others, or just from staying on the treadmill. As their roles shift and doubts about their identities grow, reinvention may be beyond consideration. In addition, because previous generations retired earlier, didn't live as long, and didn't have access to the gig economy, many couples lack role models for what reinvention can look like at this stage of life. If they don't deliberately broaden their horizons, they miss opportunities to discover themselves anew.

So couples must explore again. Even more than in the second transition, they need to flirt with multiple possibilities. Like healthy children, who are curious about the world, themselves, and those around them, they can actively seek new experiences and experiment, avoid taking things for granted, and constantly ask "Why?" Most of us suppress our childhood curiosity as life progresses and responsibilities pile up. But it is vital to overcome the fear of leaving behind a cherished self and allow ambitions and priorities to diversify. Exploring at this stage is rejuvenating.

Shifts in people's roles and identities offer a perfect excuse to question their current work, life, and loves. Many people associate exploring with looking for new options, which is surely important. But it's also about questioning assumptions and approaches and asking, "Is this really how things need to be?"

Having rebalanced their support for each other, Norah and Jeremy could open up to new possibilities. Having earned financial security from their previous work, they sought reinvention not only in their careers but also in their wider roles in the world. Encouraging each other, they both transitioned to portfolio working lives. Jeremy became a freelance digital visual artist, took a part-time role teaching young art students at a local college, and dedicated more time to his passion of dinghy sailing. Norah retrained to be a counselor working with distressed families and began volunteering at a local agricultural museum. With these new opportunities and more time for each other and their friends, they felt newfound satisfaction with their work and with their relationship.

The challenges couples face at each transition are different but linked. In their first transition, the partners accommodate to a major life event by negotiating the roles they will play in each other's lives. Over time those roles become constraining and spark the restlessness and questioning that lead to the second transition. To successfully navigate the third transition, couples must address regrets and developmental asymmetries left over from their first two transitions.

No one right path or solution exists for meeting these challenges. Although the 50/50 marriage—in which housework and child care are divided equally between the partners, and their careers are perfectly synced—may seem like a noble ideal, my research suggests that instead of obsessively trying to maintain an even "score," dual-career couples are better off being relentlessly curious, communicative, and proactive in making choices about combining their lives.

Originally published in September–October 2019. Reprint R1905B

Cultivating Everyday Courage

by James R. Detert

IN MANY STORIES we hear about workplace courage, the people who fight for positive change end up being ostracized—and sometimes even lose their jobs. What I've seen in the course of my research, though, tells a more nuanced story. Most acts of courage don't come from whistleblowers or organizational martyrs. Instead, they come from respected insiders at all levels who take action— be it campaigning for a risky strategic move, pushing to change an unfair policy, or speaking out against unethical behavior—because they believe it's the right thing to do. Their reputations and track records enable them to make more headway than those on the margins or outside the organization could. And when they manage the process well, they don't necessarily pay a high price for their actions; indeed, they may see their status rise as they create positive change.

Consider Martha (not her real name), a finance manager at a small company. For years she endured risqué comments and sexual innuendo from her boss, the company president, and she struggled with how to handle it: Should she talk to him about his behavior, or just quit? How could she protect the other women at the firm? Then, at a staff gathering, her boss grabbed her inappropriately during a light moment, thinking it was funny. Later that day, she confronted him in his office, prepared to quit if he made no changes. She told him that his behavior made her uncomfortable and was a signal to her that she'd never advance in the company because he didn't view her as an equal. She said that perhaps he was trying to promote a fun work environment, but he was failing.

Martha was terrified that he would fire her, be angry, or tell her to toughen up. But instead, to her surprise, he apologized. He was horrified that this was how she felt—and that other women in the company probably felt the same way. He praised her for speaking out when no one else had dared to. Over subsequent months, he continued to seek her guidance on the issue and made a formal apology to the staff. A year later, Martha was promoted to a VP role: an incredible position to be in for someone who once believed that the president would never promote a woman to that level.

I began investigating workplace courage after spending more than a decade studying why people so often don't speak up at work. I've found many examples of people at all levels who created positive change without ruining their careers. Their success rested primarily on a set of attitudes and behaviors that can be learned, rather than on innate characteristics. I call people who exhibit these behaviors *competently courageous* because they create the right conditions for action by establishing a strong internal reputation and by improving their fallback options in case things go poorly; they carefully choose their battles, discerning whether a given opportunity to act makes sense in light of their values, the timing, and their broader objectives; they maximize the odds of in-the-moment success by managing the messaging and emotions; and they follow up to preserve relationships and marshal commitment. These steps are useful whether you're pushing for major change or trying to address a smaller or more local issue.

Lest anyone think I'm naive, let me be clear: Of course bad things do happen when people challenge authorities, norms, and institutions. Courage, after all, is about taking worthy actions *despite the potential risk.* If no one ever got fired, was socially isolated, or suffered other consequences for a particular action, we wouldn't consider it courageous. And good outcomes are more likely to

Idea in Brief

The Challenge

Professionals who perform courageous acts—such as pushing to change a flawed policy or speaking out against unethical behavior—risk their reputations and even their jobs.

A Better Way

People who succeed in their courageous acts, or suffer fewer negative consequences, tend to exhibit certain behaviors and

attributes: They lay the groundwork for action; they carefully choose their battles; they manage messaging and emotions; and they follow up afterward.

Getting Started

A good way to learn and master competently courageous behaviors is to engage in smaller, everyday acts before proceeding to progressively more difficult ones. Above all, keep your values and purpose front and center.

come from some types of actions than from others. For example, challenging the inappropriate behavior of a colleague with whom you have a decent relationship is, all else being equal, likely to go better for you than defying the entire power structure over an unethical practice.

Among those I studied who had failed to create positive change, almost all still thought their risk-taking had been the right thing to do. They were proud they had stood up for what they believed in—but they wished they'd done so more skillfully. Following the four principles laid out here can help people at all levels improve their chances of creating positive change when they do decide to act.

Laying the Groundwork

My research shows that employees whose workplace courage produces good results have often spent months or years establishing that they excel at their jobs, that they are invested in the organization, and that they're evenhanded. They've demonstrated that they're able to stand both apart from and with those whose support they need. In doing so, they've accumulated what psychologists call idiosyncrasy credits—a stock of goodwill derived from their history of competence and conformity—which they can cash in when challenging norms or those with more power. (I've also seen the reverse: When people with a reputation for selfishness or ill will stand up for legitimately needed change, they tend to be less successful.)

Competently courageous people also work to earn the trust of those who see them as their champions. They invest in those relationships, too—engaging with people individually, taking the time to empathize with them, and helping them develop professionally.

Consider Catherine Gill, a former senior vice president of fundraising and communication at the nonprofit social investment fund Root Capital. Gill wanted to speak up about what she and colleagues saw as the organization's unintentional yet manifest internal bias against women. The issue was particularly tricky because criticizing the leadership could easily be viewed as criticizing the organization's socially conscious mission. But she was able to launch an honest—if painful—conversation with her colleagues in senior management about the organization's culture, leading to a number of concrete changes.

Gill's track record of excelling and fitting in at the organization was fundamental to her success. Over her first two years at Root Capital, she achieved consistently high performance as a fundraiser and exhibited the emotional and intellectual intelligence to navigate complex issues. She showed that she was deeply committed to the organization's mission, regularly adjusting her role to tackle the most pressing challenges and showing how various initiatives she launched were aligned with core strategic priorities. She was careful to point out when she didn't consider something a gender issue so that people on both sides would see her as fair. All that gave her the idiosyncrasy credits she needed to be heard by the leadership team. She determined the limits of what change was possible so that she wouldn't push too far and get "voted off the island." Through her work ethic, judgment, and humor, she set the stage for more visible moments of courageous action.

Sometimes things don't work out, even with the best preparation. Competently courageous people develop mechanisms to mitigate fallout. That might mean finding ways to make themselves indispensable to the organization, keeping external options open, or minimizing economic reliance on an employer. For example, former Telecom Italia leader Franco Bernabè rejected many of the perks that came with being the CEO of a major company, knowing that doing so made it easier to take risks. "If I had lost my job," he said, "and gone back to something more subdued and less glamorous—well, it wouldn't have changed my life."

Choosing Your Battles

Not every opportunity to display courage is worth taking. The people I've studied who have been successful in their courageous acts asked themselves two questions before moving ahead: Is this really important? and, Is this the right time?

Importance, of course, lies in the eye of the beholder. It depends on your goals and values and those of your colleagues, stakeholders, and the organization itself. As you gauge whether an issue is truly important, be aware of your emotional triggers; allow yourself to be informed but not held hostage by them. Also assess whether engaging in a potential battle—whatever the outcome might be—is likely to aid or hinder winning the war. Ask yourself, for example: Will securing resources to address this problem make it less likely that a higher-priority proposal will subsequently get funded?

Competently courageous people are masters of good timing. To avoid being seen as a broken record, they are less likely to act if they recently cashed in hard-earned idiosyncrasy credits. They observe what is going on around them, and if the timing doesn't look right, they patiently hold off. They scan the environment for events and trends that could support their efforts, making the most of an organizational change or the appearance of a new ally, for example. They stay attuned to attention cycles—to public upwellings of enthusiasm for the issue at hand. Pushing for a more globally representative strategy or leadership team, for example, was for a long time risky in many organizations; now companies are more open to tackling those issues. Unless they've concluded that taking action is necessary to preserve their sense of integrity or to plant the seed of an idea, competently courageous people don't act before those around them are ready to take them seriously.

For example, when "Mandy" joined an accessories and apparel company as a product manager, she quickly learned that one of the company's vendors was highly problematic. Its reps were rude, dishonest, and manipulative, and the product itself was subpar. However, ties between the two companies were long-standing and included a friendship between two key managers. Mandy wisely waited; she didn't suggest a change until six months later. By that point she had demonstrated her commitment to the organization, and she was better able to gauge the relationships between the people involved. She used the intervening time to collect evidence of the problems, identify alternative vendors, and quantify the improvements they could offer. When she finally did make her proposal, the VP in charge responded positively.

In some cases, conditions or events such as sagging sales or a change in leadership create urgency for courageous acts—and make them more likely to succeed. Tachi Yamada, a physician-scientist turned business leader, has been a master of seizing the day during a successful career as a senior executive in the health care sector. When Yamada became head of R&D at Smith Kline Beecham in 1999, he quickly concluded that the R&D organization needed to be restructured around disease areas or "assets" (the molecules or compounds that might eventually make it to market) rather than the traditional silos. When a merger with another pharmaceutical giant—Glaxo—was announced, he campaigned for the R&D function of the combined company to be structured in that way. The proposal didn't go over well. R&D leaders and scientists at Glaxo were particularly upset; here was the new guy from the much smaller company in the merger telling them they needed a major change. They "were pretty much aligned against me," recalls Yamada. But he knew that the timing could be used to

Further Reading

"Get the Boss to Buy In," by Susan J. Ashford and James R. Detert (HBR, January–February 2015)

"Harnessing the Science of Persuasion," by Robert B. Cialdini (HBR, October 2001)

"Conducting Difficult Conversations," by Karen Dillon in *HBR Guide to Office Politics* (HBR Press, 2014)

"The Necessary Art of Persuasion," by Jay A. Conger (HBR, May–June 1998)

"Moves That Matter: Issue Selling and Organizational Change," by Jane E. Dutton, Susan J. Ashford, Regina M. O'Neill, and Katherine A. Lawrence (*Academy of Management Journal*, 2001)

Giving Voice to Values: How to Speak Your Mind When You Know What's Right, by Mary C. Gentile (Yale University Press, 2012)

Made to Stick: Why Some Ideas Survive and Others Die, by Chip Heath and Dan Heath (Random House, 2007)

his advantage: "The merger and the thin pipeline in both companies gave me a burning platform." His push for the reorganization succeeded in part because of his ability to recognize the opportunity and capitalize on it.

Persuading in the Moment

Workplace courage is, of course, about more than preparation. Eventually you must take action. During this step, competently courageous people focus primarily on three things: framing their issue in terms that the audience will relate to, making effective use of data, and managing the emotions in the room. (See "Further Reading" for more on persuasion.) They connect their agenda to the organization's priorities or values, or explain how it addresses critical areas of concern for stakeholders. They ensure that decision makers feel included—not attacked or pushed aside.

Mel Exon, a former executive at the advertising firm Bartle Bogle Hegarty (BBH), excels at framing proposals in ways that make them attractive to those whose support she needs. For example, when Exon and a colleague first pitched the idea for an internal innovation unit—BBH Labs—to senior management, support was far from unanimous. Some executives worried that the creation of a separate innovation group would imply that parts of BBH *weren't* innovative. This was concerning in a firm that proudly considered itself the contrarian visionary in the industry, with a black sheep as its calling card.

To convince the skeptics that BBH Labs was philosophically aligned with the company's mission, Exon took advantage of internal stakeholders' pride in the black sheep image, pointing out that some of BBH's clients had come to the company specifically for groundbreaking ideas. A lab focused on innovation would fulfill exactly that need. She won over others by describing the work of the new lab as advance scouting, promising that everyone at the firm would share in its findings. Exon eventually got the go-ahead from senior management, and later BBH's CEO complimented her approach, describing it as building on the company's DNA rather than trying to change it.

Keeping your cool as you perform your courageous act can be just as important as how you make your case. A manager I'll call Erik, who was tasked with growing the solar business at one of the world's largest multinationals, frequently butted heads with senior executives in the company's traditional lines of business. When he sought their support for new business models, they often pushed back, telling him brusquely, "We don't do that" or "That will never work here." The discussions could get heated, and Erik often felt frustrated by the executives' defensiveness. But instead of taking the emotional bait, he reminded himself that their response was a normal reaction to fear of the unknown. Acknowledging their mindset helped him stay calm and concentrate on simply making data-driven arguments. In the end, he was able to bring others around to his point of view, and the business made a strong pivot toward his recommended strategy.

Following Up

Those who exhibit competent courage follow up after they take action, no matter how things turned out. They manage their relationships with the people involved: When things go well, they thank supporters and share credit. When things go badly, they address lingering emotions and repair ties with those who might be hurt or angry.

For example, Catherine Gill made an in-the-moment decision to launch her campaign to change the culture at Root Capital during a retreat with about 30 leaders present. But as a result of her spontaneous decision, she caught the CEO off guard. Knowing that the very difficult conversation that ensued might have felt to him like an indictment of his leadership—and that he might see her actions as a personal attack—Gill checked in with him privately at that evening's dinner. She assured him that she wasn't trying to start a revolution; she was trying to advance the firm's evolution into its ideal form.

Follow-up also means continuing to pursue your agenda beyond the first big moment of action. Even when their initial steps go well, the competently courageous continue to advocate, reach out to secure resources, and make sure others deliver on promises. And when things don't go well, they take it in stride, viewing setbacks as learning opportunities rather than hiding from the fallout or giving up.

Take Fred Keller, who established a welfare-to-career program at the company he founded, Cascade Engineering. In the initiative's first incarnation, participants were often late or absent, and their performance was poor. Within a few weeks, not one of the new hires remained, and Cascade's employees and supervisors were left feeling frustrated. Instead of giving up, Keller viewed the failure as an opportunity to learn. Finding that neither Cascade nor its new hires had been well prepared for the program, he reinstated it with more training for everyone involved. When this second attempt seemed headed toward a similar fate, Keller harnessed the growing criticism to get it right. He further increased training of leaders and partnered with a county official to bring a social worker on-site to work with the new hires to identify and solve problems before they escalated.

This time Keller's persistence and learning paid off: The program is now a core part of the organization and is widely lauded as a model for transitioning people from welfare to work. And through his persistence, Keller earned tremendous loyalty from his staff at all levels of the company.

Getting Started

Courage isn't required only for high-stakes campaigns. My research with Evan Bruno, a PhD student at Darden, shows that a host of everyday actions require employees to act courageously. Sometimes simply doing one's job well requires courage. It's also worth noting that "risk" encompasses more than the prospect of financial ruin or getting fired. Humans naturally fear rejection, embarrassment, and all sorts of other social and economic consequences. From the outside, for example, it might be easy to question whether Fred Keller's actions required courage. As the owner of the company, Keller could do whatever he wanted, so where's the risk? But for years, he faced doubters both inside and outside his organization. To persevere knowing that people might think he was a "nutcase" or that he was wasting time or money took courage.

The good news is that the experiences of those I've studied show that competently courageous behaviors can be learned. They're dependent on effort and practice, rather than on some heroic personality trait limited to the few. (So don't use that as an excuse to let yourself off the hook if you find yourself in a situation that calls for courage!) One piece of advice I give to students and clients: Don't jump into the deep end right away. Instead, approach this work incrementally by trying smaller, more manageable acts before proceeding to progressively harder ones. That might mean having a difficult conversation in some other sphere of life, or broaching a tough topic with a colleague you like and respect, before confronting a boss about demeaning behavior. It might mean guiding your own team in a new direction before suggesting a transformation of the whole organization. And consider what "small" means to you—we all have different perceptions of which actions require courage. (To see how your perception of what takes courage lines up with others', take our Workplace Courage Acts Index self-assessment at www.workplacecai.com.) Then, as you tackle each step, focus on what you learn, not whether it goes perfectly the first time.

Above all, keep your values and purpose front and center. You'll have a stronger sense of self-respect through any setbacks you face, and you'll be less likely to regret your actions, no matter how things turn out. And by using the principles discussed in this article, you'll increase the chances of successfully creating change, making the risks you take all the more worthwhile.

Originally published in November–December 2018. Reprint R1806K

How to Call Out Racial Injustice at Work

by James R. Detert and Laura Morgan Roberts

In a time of intense pain, anger, and collective attention around issues of racial injustice, many people—African Americans especially—are seizing the moment to speak truth to power at work. They are holding senior leaders accountable for their commitments to increased diversity; confronting colleagues or clients who make insensitive or ignorant comments; and calling out those who mock the Black Lives Matter movement or dismiss calls for justice and human rights.

Speaking up is risky, but studies have shown that confronting injustice of any kind is also vitally important. It's key to our individual and collective well-being, learning, and, ultimately, organizational performance.

So how can you take a stand for advancing racial justice in your own organization, while also improving your chances for leading change from within, mitigating risk of rejection, and preserving your career options and mental health?

Speaking out at work is difficult, especially when those above us are implicated in some way. We fear—for good reason—that we'll suffer career, social, psychological, or other kinds of harm for being honest about discrimination. Even the suggestion of racist behavior directly challenges a person's integrity, increasing the risk of an explosive or defensive response. Thus, people who champion diversity face a host of negative consequences because of widespread resistance to targeted efforts to promote equity and inclusion.

As high as the stakes are for white people who speak up, they're higher if you're Black. Raise these issues with white colleagues and you risk being seen as biased, overly emotional (for example, too angry), and a host of other negative stereotypes that may have little to do with the problem you're trying to address. Here's an insidious example from one of us (Jim). In one of my classes, I present students with a story of a Black manager who is called a racial slur by a white subordinate and I ask what the Black boss should do. Students typically advise this manager to turn to HR for help so he won't be perceived as unfair in his discipline of a white subordinate. Asked what they would tell the manager if he were white, some of the same students see him as capable of taking disciplinary action against a subordinate of any race without help.

Courageous actions are rooted in people's willingness to sacrifice their security and stability for the sake of a cause that is greater than their career advancement. But that doesn't mean that you should be cavalier about raising issues of racial justice. Here are five strategies to help you maximize your impact when speaking truth to power at work.

Use Allies and Speak as a Collective

Find like-minded colleagues and raise an issue together. People we studied reported that speaking up as a group about workplace issues was more effective than going it alone because a group can't be written off as "one disgruntled person." Collective voice is especially impactful when it comes from a multicultural coalition of allies. It's harder to dismiss non-Black allies on the grounds that they're being biased or self-interested, and a unified front shows that Black issues are human issues, important to everyone in the community. If you can't find like-minded collaborators within your company, use social proof by pointing to others who share your point of view (ideally, choose someone whose views are deeply respected by your target audience).

Examples of groups that have applied collective pressure for anti-racist institutional change include Google employees, who filed a petition demanding that the company stop selling software to police units; and members of Kansas State's college football team, who refused to play until the school met their demands for demonstrating accountability for racist actions on campus.

Channel Your Emotions (but Don't Suppress Them)

Revealing the full extent of your rage or despair in front of those with power sets you up to be dismissed or punished for being "too emotional." It's completely justifiable to be angry (outraged), hurt, and sad about the infractions you've witnessed. (We are too.) And you shouldn't ignore these strong emotions: Find safe spaces to help you honor them so that you can channel them as energy that fuels your next steps—conversations with confidantes, for example, or with counselors. Then, after you are feeling centered, you might call attention to the racial injustice that occurred.

Here's an example. Terrence, a young Black man, confronted his significantly older, white boss about using racial slurs at work. It was a bold move for Terrence to call out this behavior in public given the hierarchical nature of the place and the knowledge that there were "a lot of racist people working there in higher positions." Despite the strong emotions he felt, Terrence spoke in a firm and measured way, showing compassion and a desire to help correct behavior rather than shame or scold his boss. This allowed his boss to see the ignorance and hurtfulness of his statements and, according to one of Terrence's colleagues, led him to change his ways, rather than reacting defensively.

Anticipate Others' Negative Reactions

As much as this feels like a time to focus on your own feelings of out-
rage and pain, you should also anticipate strong emotional reactions
from the people you're confronting. Demanding improvements in
racial equity stands a good chance of evoking defensiveness and
fear. Inquiry and framing can help to defuse negative reactions and
align shared goals.

For example, if your request evokes a furrowed brow or a crossing
of arms across the chest, start asking questions: "These seem like
appropriate next steps to me, but perhaps they feel problematic to
you. Can you help me understand what you're thinking, and why
these may not seem right to you?" You don't have to agree with what
is said next, but your effort to acknowledge that your counterpart
has feelings too can increase your chance of reaching a mutually sat-
isfactory outcome.

Frame What You Say So It's Compelling to Your Counterpart

Delivering your message as inclusively as possible can help with the
sense of divisiveness often associated with calls for racial justice.
Make it easier for those you're imploring to change to see your message as coming from a position of "We are evolving together" rather
than "I am revolting against you." This framing highlights collective
progress, which—even when modest—helps people to cultivate
positive identities and to find meaning and persistence to conquer
challenges of all kinds at work, from diversity and inclusion initiatives to other projects that require people to come together. If possible, make note of at least one way your organization has already
made progress on racial inclusion (such as holding a town hall Q&A,
making a public statement, establishing task forces, or investing in
minority business enterprises) and try to build from there.

When you're trying to compel others to act differently, especially
those above you, it's also critical to use language that will resonate
with them, rather than relying on arguments that are meaningful

only to you. When advocating for change, for instance, many of us lead with economic or instrumental arguments. However, in many cases, that might not be the best strategy. Arguing for racial equity on the sole basis of financial gain suggests that basic justice and decency toward people of all races is optional unless it can be proven to have some economic value. It's not optional, and requiring people of color to justify their demands for basic human rights in this degrading manner is yet another injury inflicted upon them.

You can reframe this moral imperative in a way that resonates with your audience, however. If, for example, your boss is motivated by external threats, explain how your proposals will keep customers who are disgusted by your company's lack of action from abandoning you. If your boss is more excited by opportunities, talk about how embracing equality and inclusion will attract customers and top talent.

Follow Up

After a difficult conversation, the last thing we want to do is to reengage anytime soon. But no matter how well you handled yourself in the first encounter, these topics are so sensitive that there's a decent chance that someone left the discussion feeling personally indicted or misunderstood. If you need the people you've confronted to stand with you for real change to take root, you'll want to check in.

Start by acknowledging the difficulty of the subject: "I know our conversation was a really tough one, and I imagine it could have left you with lingering feelings. Can we talk about that?" That can be a powerful way to move forward together and also gives you the opportunity to clarify misunderstandings and to nail down details like resource commitments, action steps, and agreements on measurement and accountability that can give your call for change a better chance of real success.

Our aim in providing this advice is not to place an additional burden on people of color, who already must deal with the unfair weight of their counterparts' hurt feelings even as they themselves are targets of injustice. Instead we acknowledge the reality of those burdens and the uneven distribution of that racial work and hope to give people of color and their allies greater agency, discretion, and impact in the ongoing fight for change. In so doing, we also aim to lessen the repercussions of speaking out about racial injustice for people's well-being and careers.

A final thought about the courage it takes to speak up in the workplace about racial injustice: If you have attempted to implement these suggestions and still see little to no progress, take stock of where you are and where you wish to be. It might be time to look around your organization for a new team or assignment with leaders and allies who are willing to join you in this work. Or, it might be time for you to find a new organization where you employ your talents among those more demonstrably committed to the changes you seek.

Adapted from content originally published in July 2020. Reprint H05QRG

How Men Can Become Better Allies to Women

by W. Brad Johnson and David G. Smith

When men are deliberately engaged in gender-inclusion programs, the evidence shows that 96% of organizations see progress—compared to only 30% of organizations where men are not engaged. But too many organizations miss the mark on gender-equity efforts by focusing gender initiatives solely on changing women—from the way they network to the way they lead. Individualistic approaches to solving gender inequities overlook systemic structural causes and reinforce the perception that these are women's issues—effectively telling men they don't need to be involved. Without the avid support of men—often the most powerful stakeholders in most large corporations—significant progress toward ending gender disparities is unlikely. What's at stake? A study by McKinsey projects that in a "full potential" scenario in which women participate in the economy identically to men, $28 trillion (26%) would be added to the annual global GDP when compared to the current business-as-usual scenario.

But engaging men in diversity efforts is not as simple as inviting them to a one-off gender-equity event. In order to overcome the reluctance and anxiety these efforts often produce and to achieve real, systemic change, we must begin from the understanding that although sexism is a system that privileges men, it also polices male behavior.

Challenges Facing Male Allies

We define male allies as members of an advantaged group committed to building relationships with women, expressing as little sexism in their own behavior as possible, understanding the social privilege conferred by their gender, and demonstrating active efforts to address gender inequities at work and in society.

While some research has shown that white men face no penalty for promoting diversity, other studies suggest that there can be a cost to acting as an ally.

First, there's the dreaded "wimp penalty." New research reveals that men perceived as less self-promoting and more collaborative and power sharing are evaluated by both men and women as less competent (and, not incidentally, less masculine). This is more likely to occur in organizations where people endorse a zero-sum perspective on gender equality.

Self-professed male allies can also face criticism from the women they try to ally with. As two men who write and speak about cross-gender allyship and mentorship, we've witnessed occasional backlash when dudes show up at gender-equity events. Women at one conference circulated a Bingo card just before a panel composed of men on the topic of allyship. The objective? To identify as many worn-out clichés and defensive phrases men often utter in these contexts as possible. Some eye-rolling favorites included: "I'm a feminist." "We're all in this together." "My mother taught me to respect women." "I saw the light after the birth of my daughter!"

There are many legitimate reasons for women to be skeptical of men's participation and motives. For one thing, women's conferences and employee resource groups have historically offered women a sense of community and camaraderie, a safe space for sharing experiences and formulating strategies for addressing inequality in the workplace. Then there are the subtracks and breakout sessions labeled "Manbassador" or "Male Champion," which are terrific for drawing men in but sound grandiose to women, who may rightfully ask, "Really? We have to call you a champion just to get you to be fair, respectful, and inclusive?"

This "pedestal effect" in which men are given special treatment for even small acts of gender equality is understandably grating for women who for years have done the emotional labor and carried the load for equality, with nary a man in sight. And there is always the risk that overfocusing on men in women's events may ultimately strengthen rather than dismantle the gender-hierarchy status quo.

There is also the problem of the "fake male feminist" who slings on feminism like a superhero cape when his boss is watching, to impress— or worse, seduce—women, or to avoid being labeled as sexist despite a pattern of sexist behavior. And the sincere but utterly naive, ill-informed, or low-EQ man whose notion of allyship amounts to rescuing, mansplaining, or even attempting to become the spokesman for women in the organization. As Martin Luther King, Jr., once reflected, "Shallow understanding from people of good will is more frustrating than absolute misunderstanding from people of ill will." When aspiring male allies fail to understand the critical importance of partnering and collaborating with humility, there is a real risk that they may ultimately undermine women's initiatives by attempting to dominate them.

The Allies Male Allies Need

Women who want to dismantle sexist systems will be well served by appreciating the variation among male allies and the factors most likely to help those allies improve at collaborating with women to shrink gender disparities. Diversity consultant Jennifer Brown frames male allyship on a continuum, ranging from *apathetic* (clueless and disinterested regarding gender issues) to *aware* (has some grasp of the issues but not at all active or engaged in addressing them) to *active* (well informed and willing to engage in gender-equity efforts, but only when asked) to *advocate* (routinely and proactively champions gender inclusion). Although we wouldn't waste our time recruiting apathetic men to gender-inclusion events, we're delighted to get in a room with the other three varieties, taking a shot at spurring their internal motivation and sharpening their ally skill set. We need them in the fight! And evidence shows that the more positive interaction men have with women in professional settings, the less prejudice and exclusion they tend to demonstrate.

Organizers of gender-equity initiatives who wish to engage male allies might also benefit from recent research on psychological standing (perceived legitimacy that comes from being seen as an ally to women). Evidence reveals that gender-parity efforts are most effective when men believe they have an honorable and important role to play, that transformation in the workplace is something they can share in. Men are often inspired to take on this role when they hear stories of discrimination that violate their sense of fairness and justice from women whom they know personally or professionally. Moreover, when allies feel accepted by the disadvantaged group they endeavor to support, their internal motivation to participate is bolstered.

How Men Can Be Better Allies

Here are some best practices for men who want to be better collaborators and allies for gender equality in the workplace, based on research for our book, *Good Guys: How Men Can Become Better Allies for Women in the Workplace*:

- *First, just listen!* Consultant Chuck Shelton reminds men that listening to women's voices in a way that inspires trust and respect is a fundamental relationship promise you must make, and then keep, with women when you join the fight for equity.

Generous, world-class listening requires focus, sincerity, empathy, refusal to interrupt, and genuine valuing of both her experience and her willingness to share it with you.

- *Respect the space.* Women's conferences and employee resource groups are often seen as a response to experiences of exclusion, marginalization, and discrimination. Many of these experiences are painful. Large events and local resource groups have afforded women a powerful platform for sharing experiences, providing support, and strategizing. Tread respectfully into these spaces, and before you utter a word, revisit the recommendation above.

- *Remember, it's not about you.* Ask women how you can amplify, not replace or usurp, existing gender-parity efforts. A large dose of gender humility will help here. Decades of research on prosocial (helpful) behavior reveals a stark gender difference in how it is expressed. While women often express helpfulness communally and relationally, men show helpful intentions through action-oriented behaviors. Sometimes, we need to rein this in. Refrain from taking center stage, speaking for women, or mansplaining how women should approach gender-equity efforts.

- *Get comfortable being uncomfortable.* Developing psychological standing requires a commitment to learning and advocating for gender equity. Learning about the professional challenges of women may produce feelings of self-shame or self-blame that cause anxiety. The solution is more interaction and learning, not less.

- *Engage in supportive partnerships with women.* The best cross-gender ally relationships are reciprocal, and mutually growth-enhancing. Share your social capital (influence, information, knowledge, and organizational resources) with women's groups, but ask them—don't assume you know—how you can best support their efforts.

- *Remember the two parts to allyship.* Keep in mind that committing to express as little sexism as possible in your interactions with women is the easy part of allyship. The hard part requires you to take informed action. Use your experience in events and initiatives run by women to learn how you can best become a public ally for social justice around gender. When the time comes, this may require you to upset the status quo.

Adapted from content originally published in October 2018. Reprint H04L31

Be Your Own Best Advocate

by Deborah M. Kolb

MOST SEASONED MANAGERS know how to handle formal negotiations at work—with clients over contracts, with bosses over budgets, with employers over compensation. But what about all the opportunities for informal negotiations that arise? Do you know how to recognize and seize chances to move into a better role, change an untenable situation, or ensure that you get credit for extra work?

In the 35 years I've been studying negotiation and coaching executives, I've found that many people don't. Consider the following examples:

Charlotte, a sales manager, learned through the grapevine that a regional role was opening up and wanted to be considered for it. But she'd also heard that another candidate, whom the division president knew well, was a front-runner for the job. She wondered how to put herself in contention.

Kevin, a communications director, pitched in to help another division save a major client, to great acclaim. Soon colleagues in that division kept asking him to contribute. He wasn't sure how to say no.

Marina, the CFO of a $4 billion division in a large industrial manufacturing firm, had been promoted to her job two years earlier. She'd relocated to headquarters—a requirement for taking the position—and brought her husband and children with her, but they were unhappy and wanted to move back "home." She felt she had to choose between her job and her family.

All three of these professionals (whose names have been changed) were understandably stymied. Negotiating on your own behalf can feel much less comfortable than negotiating as an agent for your company, especially when it happens outside the typical structure of a hiring or review process. More emotions are in play; it's often difficult to figure out exactly what you want or how to get the conversation started; and failure carries a higher cost. In some organizations, advocating for yourself may be seen as being demanding or not a "team player." This can be especially true for women, who are sometimes hit by what researchers call "the social cost of asking." And in some cases, the very issues you want to negotiate may challenge established ways of doing work.

But executives hurt themselves if they ignore everyday opportunities to push for better assignments, goals, or performance measures; more resources or flexibility; or higher compensation. I've found that these types of negotiations, which I call "lowercase n" negotiations, matter just as much as formal, "N" negotiations. They can drive career success and fulfillment and also have the potential to spark positive organizational change.

So we all need a strategy for everyday negotiations that will allow us to come away not only successful but also still held in high regard by bosses and colleagues. I counsel those with whom I work to focus on four steps: *recognize, prepare, initiate*, and *navigate*.

Recognize

Negotiation opportunities aren't always obvious, especially if you've never thought to ask for anything in the past. But some routine situations cry out for bargaining. For example, if you say yes to a special assignment or a request for help when you want to say no, that's an opportunity to negotiate for something in return. When you're asked to take on a new initiative, with its attendant risks, that's an opportunity to negotiate for support. If your workload expands beyond what's reasonable and cuts into your family time, that's an opportunity to negotiate for more resources or to change the scope

Idea in Brief

Most seasoned managers know how to handle formal negotiations at work: with clients over contracts, with bosses over budgets, with employers over compensation. But what about the opportunities for informal negotiation that arise? Do you know how to recognize and seize the chances you get to position yourself for a better role, change an untenable situation, or ensure that you're getting credit for extra work? Many people don't, and the reason is understandable.

Negotiating as an agent for your organization can feel more comfortable than negotiating on your own behalf. More emotions are at play; it's often difficult to figure out exactly what you want or how to get the conversation started; and the risk of failure carries a higher cost. Sometimes advocating for oneself is seen as not being a "team player." But leaders hurt themselves if they ignore opportunities to push for better assignments, more resources, or higher compensation. They can successfully make their case by focusing on four steps: *recognize, prepare, initiate,* and *navigate.*

of your role. You must pick your battles, though. The issue should be important to you, but your desired outcome should not only benefit you personally but also benefit your organization, as a result of your increased productivity and commitment and new cultural norms that allow colleagues to achieve the same. The decision to negotiate should be made with a sense of the end in mind.

Initially, Marina didn't even consider talking to her boss, Robert, the company's CFO, about an arrangement that would allow her to both keep her job and live with her family. She focused on all the obstacles—lack of precedent, presumed resistance—and never imagined an ideal scenario. She conceded the negotiation without even starting it.

Kevin at first thought he needed to respond yes or no to the other division's continued requests for help, rather than contrive a "yes-and" solution: *Yes,* he would do the work, *and* in order to do it well he would need his boss to officially broaden his role to include the new responsibilities.

Prepare

Preparation is critical to any negotiation. But how can you prepare for an informal one that your counterpart isn't expecting?

First, gather good information

The more you know about what others have asked for and been granted at work, the more comfortable you'll feel crafting your own negotiation. Marina didn't think her company had ever allowed anyone to do a "headquarters job" out of another office, but she decided to check. She learned that one executive had indeed been given permission to work remotely for six weeks while he was helping to manage a family illness. When Charlotte asked around, she learned that her organization was in the early stages of considering who might fill the regional role; the other candidate didn't yet have a lock on the job.

You also need intelligence on the parties with whom you'll be negotiating. How do they like to receive news or special requests? Do they want a lot of advance notice? Do they want you to present a solution or to develop one with you?

Robert hadn't hired Marina; in fact, they'd worked together for less than a year. But she knew that he tended to resist unconventional ideas and practices; he liked the usual way of doing things. So she understood that she'd have to enter her negotiation slowly and be ready for pushback. Charlotte, too, realized early on that she had an uphill climb because Michael, the division president, already had a favorite in mind, but she learned as much as she could both about the job requirements and the qualities Michael valued most in his employees and about his decision-making style.

Second, position yourself

Interdependence gives people a reason to negotiate. So look at how your work enables your counterpart and others to succeed; that will help you discern what he or she values in you and assess yourself in a currency that matters. Marina knew that Robert appreciated the work she'd done in her divisional role. She'd achieved significant profit growth, managed a difficult labor negotiation, overseen an important acquisition, and aggressively pursued cost reductions. Since Robert was new to the company, she was also his "lifeline" to the leaders in her large division. All this gave her leverage.

Another way to think about your value proposition and your relative bargaining position is to consider your—and your partner's—"best alternative to a negotiated agreement," or BATNA (as Roger Fisher and William Ury call it in *Getting to Yes*). Kevin's BATNA was to stop putting in extra time for the other division and return to his "day job"; his colleagues and boss had weaker BATNAs, because they had nobody as well suited as Kevin to do the relevant work. Marina's BATNAs weren't very appealing: She didn't want to live apart from her family, and she wasn't confident that she could find a job as good as her current one in her previous hometown. But her boss's BATNA wasn't good either. There were no obvious candidates who could take on her role and be as successful as she'd been.

Third, anchor with options

Negotiations require creativity. When you present many ideas, you're framing the negotiation in a way that encourages the other party to join. You shouldn't fixate on a single solution that works for you. Instead consider what matters to your counterpart and find multiple ways to satisfy both of you.

In developing options, it helps to think what good reasons your counterpart might have for saying no to an arrangement you propose. These are on the hidden agenda of any negotiation.

Charlotte knew from her information gathering that Michael would probably balk at her youth and inexperience in comparison with his favored candidate and suggest that she needed more seasoning in her current role before taking on a new one. So she broadened her proposals to include volunteering to perform the role in an "acting" capacity for a limited period of time, with clear performance benchmarks, or taking another developmental opportunity that would put her more firmly on a leadership track.

Marina was sure that Robert would be concerned about breaking from precedent, the incremental expense of a flexible arrangement, and losing touch with her and her division. So she rejected ideas that would heighten those concerns—such as working from home and coming in to headquarters only for meetings—and focused on ones that would assuage them, such as splitting her time between her old divisional office and HQ. She also pulled together a spreadsheet of estimated expenses. These preparations not only boosted her confidence but also helped her appreciate Robert's point of view and put her in the right mindset to work on a joint solution.

Initiate

Any two people typically feel asymmetrical desires to engage in everyday negotiations. One has a problem or sees an opportunity; the other probably doesn't and therefore expects business as usual. How can you shift a normal interaction into a collaborative rather than combative negotiation?

Start by making your value visible. When Marina decided to approach Robert about her work-family conflict, she didn't begin the conversation with it. She first reviewed her results since their previous meeting and updated him on a recent acquisition. Only then did she mention her problem and begin to talk about ideas for solving it.

If the other party stonewalls, you can consider various tactics. One is to round up allies who will vouch for your value and encourage the person to negotiate with you. Because Charlotte didn't know Michael very well, she enlisted another leader in the division to extol her virtues and the contributions she was making to the company.

Another approach is to acknowledge and address one or more of your counterpart's good reasons for saying no to prove that you've thought about his or her perspective. Often the response will be "Right, this is my concern," which opens the door to a conversation about the issue. Marina chose this path. Her boss's most legitimate fear was that he would lose his connection to the division. So she gave him a chance to discuss it by saying, "I can see why you might be concerned about this. That's why one of the options I thought about was dual offices."

You can also introduce a BATNA, but you must do so carefully, so it's not perceived as a threat. You might mention yours and then retract it. For example, Marina could have told Robert that she was getting calls from headhunters (which was true) but then quickly noted that she was committed to staying at the company if he and she could work out a plan. To make your counterpart more aware of his or her own BATNA, ask a question such as "What do you think will happen if we don't have this conversation?"

Navigate

Once you've enticed the other party to engage in a negotiation, you must go into the conversation with an open mind. The proposals you're prepared to offer are just starting points for an agreement. Three types of questions can help the two of you develop a plan that works for everyone.

Hypothesis-testing questions start with "What if" and enable you to introduce ideas, whether broad or specific, and solicit a reaction. For example, Marina asked Robert, "What if we created dual offices? How would that work?" As the discussion progressed, she got more detailed: "What if we had a shared calendar, so you knew exactly where I would be when? What if you had the opportunity to be involved in certain divisional meetings?" Kevin, too, used this kind of question to great effect in his conversations with colleagues in the other division. When he asked, "What if I couldn't do this work?" he learned that they would be at a complete loss and were therefore willing to support him in negotiations with his boss, Dorothy, about taking formal responsibility over work in their domain.

Reciprocity questions involve if-then scenarios and build the notion of trading into the negotiation: "If I agree to do X, then what will you do?" Marina used this type of question to navigate the issue of costs with her boss: "If we agree to the dual-office arrangement, what else do you need?" Ultimately they decided that she would pay for a reverse relocation, but the company would absorb the ongoing travel expenses. When Kevin approached Dorothy, his if-then scenario was "If I work with the other division on an ongoing basis, here is how it could become part of my new and expanded senior director's role."

Moves and Turns

WHEN NEGOTIATORS DON'T WANT TO GIVE YOU what you're asking for, they often launch an offensive move. Don't get defensive. Instead, turn the conversation to get it back on track.

When he challenges your ability—"I don't think you're ready"—correct his impression: "I understand why it might appear that way. But here's the experience I have that shows why I'm capable of managing it . . ."

When she demeans your ideas as unreasonable—"That will never work"—divert her focus to the solution: "What would be a reasonable arrangement?"

When he appeals for sympathy—"It's such a tough time for this group right now"—dig deeper: "What really concerns you? What can I do to ease those concerns?"

When she criticizes your approach—"This is a really inappropriate request"—ask for elaboration: "Can you help me understand why?"

When he flatters you—"You're so good in the position you have"—use a role reversal: "If you were in my shoes, what would you do?"

Another turn that works against almost any move is to interrupt the conversation by sitting silent for a brief period, standing up, or moving to get a glass of water. Research shows that when you break the action, people rarely revert to the same negotiating stance, and the pause can lead to breakthroughs.

Circular questions, which simultaneously introduce and gather information, ensure that the conversation is collaborative, not adversarial. They emphasize the relationship between you and your counterpart and often unearth deeper issues at stake. Charlotte knew that simply asking for the role she wanted would put Michael in an awkward position. So she asked circular questions such as "What are the success criteria for this job?" Michael then considered more deeply what he was looking for, which opened the process up to more candidates. Marina used circular questions such as "What really concerns you?" and "What can I do to ease those concerns?" with Robert. It turned out that he feared the plan would fail because she might find the constant commuting too difficult. "I promised him that if that happened, we would work something out, even if it was an exit strategy," she says. "He would not be left high and dry."

She also proposed that they agree to a six-month trial of the dual-office arrangement and then jointly assess the results.

All three of these executives were successful in their negotiations. Marina and her family moved back home, but she stayed in her job. The dual-office arrangement worked, so Robert agreed to make it permanent, establishing a precedent for senior executives to be based where they could be most effective and of most value to the company—not necessarily at headquarters. Kevin's job was restructured to include additional staff so that he could work with the new clients. Charlotte got the regional manager's job and prompted Michael to be more explicit about the criteria used for promotion in his division.

Everyday negotiations often require you to leave your comfort zone and challenge established practices. But all evidence indicates that they're worth the effort—for you and for your organization.

Originally published in November 2015. Reprint R1511J

Building an Ethical Career

by Maryam Kouchaki and Isaac H. Smith

MOST OF US THINK of ourselves as good people. We set out to be ethical, and we hope that in pivotal moments we will rise to the occasion. But when it comes to building an ethical career, good intentions are insufficient. Decades' worth of research has identified social and psychological processes and biases that cloud people's moral judgment, leading them to violate their own values and often to create contorted, post hoc justifications for their behavior. So how can you ensure that from day to day and decade to decade you will do the right thing in your professional life?

The first step requires shifting to a mindset we term *moral humility*—the recognition that we all have the capacity to transgress if we're not vigilant. Moral humility pushes people to admit that temptations, rationalizations, and situations can lead even the best of us to misbehave, and it encourages them to think of ethics as not only avoiding the bad but also pursuing the good. It helps them see this sort of character development as a lifelong pursuit. We've been conducting research on morality and ethics in the workplace for more than a decade, and on the basis of our own and others' findings, we suggest that people who want to develop ethical careers should consider a three-stage approach: (1) Prepare in advance for moral challenges; (2) make good decisions in the moment; and (3) reflect on and learn from moral successes and failures.

Planning to Be Good

Preparing for ethical challenges is important, because people are often well aware of what they *should* do when thinking about the future but tend to focus on what they *want* to do in the present. This tendency to overestimate the virtuousness of our future selves is part of what Ann Tenbrunsel of Notre Dame and colleagues call *the ethical mirage.*

Counteracting this bias begins with understanding your personal strengths and weaknesses. What are your values? When are you most likely to violate them? In his book *The Road to Character,* David Brooks distinguishes between *résumé* virtues (skills, abilities, and accomplishments that you can put on your résumé, such as "increased ROI by 10% on a multimillion-dollar project") and *eulogy* virtues (things people praise you for after you've died, such as being a loyal friend, kind, and a hard worker). Although the two categories may overlap, résumé virtues often relate to what you've done for yourself, whereas eulogy virtues relate to the person you are and what you've done for others—that is, your character.

So ask yourself: What eulogy virtues am I trying to develop? Or, as the management guru Peter Drucker asked, "What do you want to be remembered for?" and "What do you want to contribute?" Framing your professional life as a quest for contribution rather than achievement can fundamentally change the way you approach your career. And it's helpful to consider those questions early, before you develop mindsets, habits, and routines that are resistant to change.

Goal setting can also lay the groundwork for ethical behavior. Professionals regularly set targets for many aspects of their work and personal lives, yet few think to approach ethics in this way. Benjamin Franklin famously wrote in his autobiography about trying to master 13 traits he identified as essential for a virtuous life (including industry, justice, and humility). He even created a chart to track his daily progress. We don't suggest that everyone engage in similarly rigid documentation, but we do suggest that you sit down and write out eulogy-virtue goals that are challenging but attainable. That is similar

Idea in Brief

Most of us think of ourselves as good people. We set out to be ethical at work, and we hope that in pivotal moments we will rise to the occasion. But when it comes to building an ethical career, good intentions are insufficient. Decades' worth of research has identified psychological processes and biases that cloud people's moral judgment, leading them to violate their own values, and often to create contorted, post hoc justifications for their behavior.

How can we ensure that we will consistently do the right thing in

our professional lives? By shifting our mindset to one of *moral humility*, recognizing that we all have the capacity for ethical transgressions if we aren't vigilant. The authors suggest a three-stage approach for staying on the straight and narrow: Prepare in advance for moral challenges, including instituting proper safeguards; make good decisions in the moment; and reflect on and learn from moral successes and failures.

to what Clayton Christensen of Harvard Business School advocated in his HBR article "How Will You Measure Your Life?" After battling cancer, Christensen decided that the metric that mattered most to him was "the individual people whose lives I've touched."

Even the most carefully constructed goals, however, are still just good intentions. They must be fortified by personal safeguards—that is, habits and tendencies that have been shown to bring out people's better angels. For instance, studies suggest that quality sleep, personal prayer (for the religious), and mindfulness can help people manage and strengthen their self-control and resist temptation at work.

We also recommend "if-then planning"—what the psychologist Peter Gollwitzer calls *implementation intentions*. Dozens of research studies have shown that this practice ("If X happens, then I will do Y") can be effective in changing people's behavior, especially when such plans are voiced aloud. They can be simple but must also be specific, tying a situational cue (a trigger) to a desired behavior. For example: *If* my boss asks me to do something potentially unethical, *then* I will turn to a friend or a mentor outside the organization for advice before acting. *If* I am solicited for a bribe, *then* I will consult my company's legal team and formal policies for guidance. *If* I witness sexual harassment or racial prejudice, *then* I will immediately stand up for the victim. Making if-then plans tailored to your strengths, weaknesses, values, and circumstances can help protect you against lapses in self-control, or inaction when action is required. But be sure to make your if-then plans *before* you encounter the situation—preparation is key.

Mentors, too, can help you avoid ethical missteps. When expanding your professional network and developing relationships with advisers, don't look only for those who can hasten your climb up the career ladder; also consider who might be able to support you when it comes to moral decisions. Build connections with people inside and outside your organization whose values are similar to yours and whom you can ask for ethics-related advice. Both of us have reached out to mentors for advice on ethical issues, and we teach our MBA students to do the same. Having a supportive network—and particularly a trusted ethical mentor—may also bring you opportunities to make a positive impact in your career.

Once you've made a commitment to living an ethical life, don't be shy about letting people know it. No one likes a holier-than-thou attitude, but subtle moral signaling can be helpful, particularly when it's directed at colleagues. You can do this by openly discussing potential moral challenges and how you would want to react or by building a reputation for doing things the right way. For example, in a study one of us (Maryam) conducted, participants were much less likely to ask an online partner to engage in unethical behavior after receiving an e-mail from that partner with a virtuous quotation in the signature line (such as "Success without honor is worse than fraud").

Direct conversation can be tricky, given that people are often hesitant to discuss ethically charged issues. But if you think it's possible, we recommend engaging your coworkers, because ambiguity is a breeding ground for self-interested rationalization. Tactfully ask clarifying questions and make your own expectations clear: for example, "I think it's important that we don't cross any ethical lines here."

We are all shaped more by our environment than we realize, so it's also critical to choose a workplace that will allow if not encourage you to behave ethically. Not surprisingly, employees who feel that their needs, abilities, and values fit well with their organization tend to be more satisfied and motivated than their misaligned peers, and they perform better. Of course, many factors go into choosing a job—but in general people tend to overemphasize traditional metrics such as compensation and promotion opportunities and underemphasize the importance of the right *moral* fit. Our work and that of others has shown that ethical stress is a strong predictor of employee fatigue, decreased job satisfaction, lower motivation, and increased turnover.

Some industries seem to have cultural norms that are more or less amenable to dishonesty. In one study, when employees of a large international bank were reminded of their professional identity, they tended to cheat more, on average, than nonbanker counterparts given the same reminder. This is not to say, of course, that all bankers are unethical, or that only unethical people should pursue careers in banking (although it does highlight how important it is for banks to prioritize hiring morally upstanding employees). We do suggest, however, that anyone starting a new job should learn about the organization and the relevant industry so as to prepare for morally compromising situations. Job interviews often conclude with the candidate's being asked, "Do you have any questions for me?" A possible response is "What types of ethical dilemmas might be faced in this job?" or "What does this company do to promote ethical business practices?"

Research also shows that elements of a work environment can enhance or diminish self-control, regardless of cultural norms: High uncertainty, excessive cognitive demands, long days and late nights, and consecutive stretch goals all correlate with increased rates of unethical behavior. Such pressures may wax and wane over time in your workplace, but during periods of intensity you should be extra vigilant.

Making Good Decisions

Even if you've planned for an ethical career and established safeguards, it can be difficult to face moral challenges in the moment. Sometimes people overlook the implications of their decisions—or they find fanciful ways of rationalizing immoral, self-interested behavior. In other instances, they face quandaries in which the right decision isn't obvious—for example, a choice between loyalty to one's coworkers and loyalty to a customer, or a proposed solution that will produce both positive and negative externalities, such as good jobs but also environmental damage. There are several ways to manage moments of truth like these.

First, step back from traditional calculations such as cost-benefit analysis and ROI. Develop a habit of searching for the moral issues and ethical implications at stake in a given decision and analyze them using multiple philosophical perspectives. For instance, from the rule-based perspective of deontology (the study of moral obligation), ask yourself what rules or principles are relevant. Will a certain course of action lead you to violate the principle of being honest or of respecting others? From the consequence-based perspective of utilitarianism, identify potential outcomes for all parties involved or affected either directly or indirectly. What is the greatest good for the greatest number of people? And from the Aristotelian perspective of virtue ethics, ask yourself, Which course of action would best reflect a virtuous person? Each of these philosophies has advantages and disadvantages, but addressing the fundamental decision criteria of all three—rules, consequences, and virtues—will make you less likely to overlook important ethical considerations.

Note, however, that the human mind is skilled at justifying morally questionable behavior when enticed by its benefits. We often tell ourselves things such as "Everyone does this," "I'm just following my boss's orders," "It's for the greater good," "It's not like I'm robbing a bank," and "It's their own fault—they deserve it." Three tests can help you avoid self-deceptive rationalizations.

1. *The publicity test.* Would you be comfortable having this choice, and your reasoning behind it, published on the front page of the local newspaper?

2. *The generalizability test.* Would you be comfortable having your decision serve as a precedent for all people facing a similar situation?

3. *The mirror test.* Would you like the person you saw in the mirror after making this decision—is that the person you truly want to be?

If the answer to any of these questions is no, think carefully before proceeding.

Studies also show that people are more likely to act unethically if they feel rushed. Very few decisions must be made in the moment. Taking some time for contemplation can help put things in perspective. In a classic social psychology experiment, students at Princeton Theological Seminary were much less likely to stop and help a stranger lying helpless on the ground if they were rushing to get to a lecture they were scheduled to give—on, ironically, the biblical parable of the Good Samaritan, which is about stopping to help a stranger lying helpless on the ground. So be aware of time pressures. Minding the old adage "Sleep on it" can often help you make better moral decisions. And delaying a decision may give you time to consult your ethical mentors. If they are unavailable, practice a variation on the mirror and publicity tests: Imagine explaining your actions to those advisers. If that would make you uncomfortable, be warned.

But taking an ethical stand often requires challenging coworkers or even superiors, which can be excruciatingly difficult. The now infamous Milgram experiments (wherein study participants administered potentially lethal shocks to innocent volunteers when they were instructed to do so by an experimenter) demonstrated how susceptible people can be to pressure from others—especially those in positions of power. How can you avoid succumbing to social pressure? The authors of *The Business Ethics Field Guide* offer a few questions to ask yourself in such situations: Do they have a right to request that I do this? Would others in the organization feel the same way I do about this? What are the requesters trying to accomplish? Could it be accomplished in a different way? Can I refuse to comply in a manner that helps them save face? In general, be wary of doing anything just because "everybody else is doing it" or your boss told you to. Take ownership of your actions.

And don't forget that many ethical challenges people face at work have previously been confronted by others. As a result, companies often develop specific guidelines, protocols, and value statements. If in doubt about a certain situation, try consulting the formal policies of your organization. Does it have an established code of ethics? If not, ask your ethical mentor for guidance. And if you're dealing with something you view as clearly unethical but fear reprisal from a superior, check to see whether your organization has an ombudsman program or a whistle-blowing hotline.

Reflecting After the Fact

Learning from experience is an iterative, lifelong pursuit: A lot of growth happens after decisions are made and actions taken. Ethical people aren't perfect, but when they make mistakes, they review and reflect on them so that they can do better in the future. Indeed, a wide array of research—in fields as diverse as psychology, computer science, nursing, and education—suggests that reflection is a critical first step in learning from past personal experiences. Reflecting on both successes and failures helps people avoid not only repeated transgressions but also "identity segmentation," wherein they compartmentalize their personal and professional lives and perhaps live by a very different moral code in each.

But self-reflection has limitations. Sometimes ethical lapses are obvious; other times the choice is ambiguous. What's more, people can be hemmed in by their own perspectives as well as by their personal histories and biases. That's why we should seek the counsel of people we trust. You can approach this as you would job performance feedback: by asking specific questions, avoiding defensiveness, and expressing gratitude.

Finally, you can engage in what Amy Wrzesniewski of Yale calls *job crafting*: shaping your work experiences by proactively adapting the tasks you undertake, your workplace relationships, and even how you perceive your job, such that work becomes more meaningful and helps you fulfill your potential. You can apply job crafting to your ethical career by making bottom-up changes to your work and the way you approach it that will help you be more virtuous. For example, in some of the earliest studies on job crafting, Wrzesniewski and colleagues found that many hospital housekeepers viewed their work in a way that made them feel like healers, not janitors. They didn't just clean rooms; they helped create a peaceful healing environment. One custodian used her smile and humor to help cancer patients relax and feel more comfortable. She looked for opportunities to interact with them, believing that she could be a momentary bright spot in the darkness of their ongoing chemotherapy. She crafted her job to help her develop and cultivate eulogy virtues such as love, compassion, kindness, and loyalty.

You may feel that it isn't all that difficult to be an ethical professional. As your parents may have told you, just do the right thing. But the evidence suggests that out in the real world it becomes increasingly difficult to remain on the moral high ground. So take control of your ethical career by cultivating moral humility, preparing for challenging situations, maintaining your calm in the moment, and reflecting on how well you've lived up to your values and aspirations.

Originally published in January–February 2020. Reprint R2001L

When and How to Respond to Microaggressions

by Ella F. Washington, Alison Hall Birch, and Laura Morgan Roberts

IN U.S. WORKPLACES—and around the world—people are engaging in real conversations about race, justice, diversity, equality, and inclusion, inspired by the rise of the Black Lives Matter movement and widespread protests against unchecked brutalization of communities of color at the hands of the police. That's a good thing, hopefully paving the way for meaningful antiracist action from both individuals and organizations. But those discussions will be very uncomfortable, as they almost always are—not just for white employees and leaders who might be confronting their privilege for the first time but also for people of color, especially Black Americans, who know that candid talks with colleagues will mean they either face or need to call out "microaggressions."

These are incidents in which someone accidentally (or purposely) makes an offensive statement or asks an insensitive question. Microagressions are defined as "verbal, behavioral, and environmental indignities that communicate hostile, derogatory, or negative racial slights and insults to the target person or group." For Black people, they are ubiquitous across daily work and life. Here are a few seemingly innocuous statements that, in the context of racist assumptions and stereotypes, can be quite damaging:

- *"When I see you, I don't see color."* (signaling that the person doesn't acknowledge your Blackness or won't hold it against you)

- *"We are all one race: the human race."* (signaling that your experience as a Black person is no different from the experience of people of other races)

- *"You are so articulate."* (signaling that Black people are not usually capable of competent intellectual conversation)

- *"I see your hair is big today! Are you planning to wear it like that to the client meeting?"* (signaling that natural Black hairstyles are not professional)

- *"Everyone can succeed in society if they work hard enough."* (signaling that disparate outcomes for Black people result from laziness)

As suggested by the word, microaggressions seem small; but compounded over time, they can have a deleterious impact on an employee's experience, physical health, and psychological well-being. In fact, research suggests that subtle forms of interpersonal discrimination like microaggressions are *at least as harmful* as more-overt expressions of discrimination.

Microaggressions reinforce white privilege and undermine a culture of inclusion. The best solution is, of course, increasing awareness of microaggressions, insisting that employees stop committing them, and calling out those who do. But in the absence of those changes—and understanding that complete prevention is probably impossible—how should Black (and other marginalized) employees and managers respond to the microaggressions they face, within and outside of current discussions around race in the workplace?

There are three primary ways to react:

> *Let it go.* For a long time, the most common default response was choosing not to address offensive comments in the workplace. Because they are pervasive yet subtle, they can be

Idea in Brief

Microagressions are defined as verbal, behavioral, and environmental indignities that communicate hostile, derogatory, or negative racial slights and insults to the target person or group. For Black people, they are ubiquitous across daily work and life.

When you find yourself on the receiving end of a microaggression, you can respond in one of three ways: let it go, call it out immediately, or bring it up at a later date. How can you decide which path is right for the situation and handle the conversation if you choose to have one? First, discern what matters to you. Second, disarm the person who committed the microaggression; explain that you want to have an uncomfortable conversation. Third, challenge them to clarify their statement or action, then focus them on the negative impact it had. Finally, decide how you want to let the incident affect you.

emotionally draining to confront. Yet silence places an emotional tax on Black employees, who are left wondering what happened and why, questioning their right to feel offended, and reinforcing beliefs that they are not safe from identity devaluation at work.

Respond immediately. This approach allows the transgression to be called out and its impact explained while the details of the incident are fresh in the minds of everyone involved. Immediacy is an important component of correcting bad behavior. But this approach can be risky. The perpetrator might get defensive, leaving the target feeling like they somehow "lost control," did not show up as their best self, and will be labeled an overly sensitive whiner, a troublemaker, or the stereotypical angry Black person.

Respond later. A more tempered response is to address the perpetrator privately at a later point to explain why the microaggression was offensive. Here, the risk lies in the time lag. A follow-up conversation requires helping the person who committed the microaggression to first recall it and then to appreciate its impact. The Black employee bringing it up might be deemed petty—like someone who has been harboring resentment or holding on to "little things"—while the other party, having "meant no harm," has moved on. Such accusations are a form of racial gaslighting, which can be very damaging.

We recommend the following framework for determining which course is best for you in any given situation and then, if you decide to respond, for ensuring an effective dialogue.

Discern

Determine how much of an investment you want to make in addressing the microaggression. Do not feel pressured to respond to every incident; rather, feel empowered to do so when you decide you should. Consider:

- *The importance of the issue and the relationship.* If either is or both are important to you, avoidance is the wrong approach. Express yourself in a way that honors your care for the other party, and assert yourself in a way that acknowledges your concern about the issue.

- *Your feelings.* Microaggressions can make you doubt the legitimacy of your reactions. Allow yourself to feel what you feel, whether it's anger, disappointment, frustration, aggravation, confusion, embarrassment, exhaustion, or something else. Any emotion is legitimate and should factor into your decision about whether, how, and when to respond. With stronger negative emotions such as anger, it's often best to address the incident later. If you're confused, an immediate response might be preferable. If you're simply exhausted from the weight of working while Black, maybe it is best to let it go—meaning best for you, not for the perpetrator.

- *How you want to be perceived now and in the future.* There are consequences to speaking up and to remaining silent. Only you can determine which holds more weight for you in any specific situation.

Disarm

If you choose to confront a microaggression, be prepared to disarm the person who committed it. One reason we avoid conversations about race is that they make people defensive. Perpetrators of microaggressions typically fear being perceived—or worse, revealed—as racist. Explain that the conversation might get uncomfortable for them but that what they just said or did was uncomfortable for you. Invite them to sit alongside you in the awkwardness of their words or deeds while you get to the root of their behavior together.

Defy

Challenge the perpetrator to clarify their statement or action. Use a probing question, such as *"How do you mean that?"* This gives people a chance to check themselves as they unpack what happened. And it gives you an opportunity to better gauge the perpetrator's intent. One of the greatest privileges is the freedom not to notice you have privilege, so microaggressions are often inadvertently offensive. Acknowledge that you accept their intentions as they stated them but reframe the conversation around the impact of the microaggression. Explain how you initially interpreted it and why. If they continue to assert that they *"didn't mean it like that,"* remind them that you appreciate their willingness to clarify their intent and hope they appreciate your willingness to clarify their impact.

Decide

You control what this incident will mean for your life and work—what you will take from the interaction and what you will allow it to take from you. Black people, as well as those with various other marginalized and intersectional identities, are already subject to biased expectations and evaluations in the workplace. Life is sufficiently taxing without allowing microaggressions to bring you down. Let protecting your joy be your greatest and most persistent act of resistance.

A note of advice for non-Black allies old and new: The work of allyship is difficult. You will make mistakes as you learn—and you will always be learning. For anyone accused of committing a micro-aggression or counseling someone who has been accused, here are a few notes on how to respond:

- Remember that intent does not supersede impact.

- Seek to understand the experiences of your Black peers, bosses, and employees without making them responsible for your edification.

- Believe your Black colleagues when they choose to share their insights; don't get defensive or play devil's advocate.

- Get comfortable rethinking much of what you thought to be true about the world and your workplace and accept that you have likely been complicit in producing inequity.

Although more organizations are encouraging candid discussions on race in the workplace, we cannot ignore the historical backlash that Black employees have endured for speaking up. Cultural change takes time and intention. So while we encourage timely and strategic dialogue about microaggressions, it is ultimately up to each individual to respond in the way that is most authentic to who they are and how they want to be perceived.

Adapted from content originally published in July 2020. Reprint H05Q4G

ERIKA ANDERSEN is the founding partner of Proteus International and the author of *Growing Great Employees, Being Strategic, Leading So People Will Follow*, and the forthcoming *Be Bad First*.

JOSEPH L. BADARACCO is the John Shad Professor of Business Ethics at Harvard Business School, where he has taught courses on leadership, strategy, corporate responsibility, and management. His books on these subjects include the *New York Times* bestseller *Leading Quietly, Defining Moments*, and *Step Back: Bringing the Art of Reflection into Your Busy Life* (Harvard Business Review Press, 2020).

ALISON HALL BIRCH is an assistant professor at the College of Business at the University of Texas, Arlington (UTA), where she studies stigma-based bias, diversity management, and leadership.

JULIAN BIRKINSHAW is deputy dean and a professor of strategy and entrepreneurship at the London Business School. His most recent book is *Fast/Forward: Make Your Company Fit for the Future*.

JORDAN COHEN is an executive at LifeLabs Learning.

CHRISTINA CONGLETON is a leadership and change consultant at Axon Coaching and researches stress and the brain at the University of Denver. She holds a master's degree in human development and psychology from Harvard University.

NICK CRAIG is the president of the Authentic Leadership Institute.

ROB CROSS is the Edward A. Madden Professor of Global Leadership at Babson College and a coauthor of *The Hidden Power of Social Networks* (Harvard Business Review Press, 2004).

SUSAN DAVID is a founder of the Harvard/McLean Institute of Coaching, is on the faculty at Harvard Medical School, and is recognized as one of the world's leading management thinkers. She is author of the #1 *Wall Street Journal* bestseller, *Emotional Agility* (Avery), based on the concept named by HBR as a Management Idea of the Year. An in-demand speaker and adviser, David has worked with the senior leadership of hundreds of major organizations, including the United Nations, Ernst & Young, and the World Economic Forum.

JAMES R. DETERT is a professor of business administration and the associate dean of Executive Degree Programs and Leadership Initiatives at the University of Virginia's Darden School of Business.

SCOTT K. EDINGER is the founder of Edinger Consulting Group. His latest book is *The Hidden Leader: Discover and Develop Greatness within Your Company* (AMACOM, 2015).

JOSEPH R. FOLKMAN is the president of Zenger Folkman, a leadership development consultancy. He is a coauthor of the book *Speed: How Leaders Accelerate Successful Execution* (McGraw Hill, 2016).

W. BRAD JOHNSON is a professor of psychology in the Department of Leadership, Ethics, and Law at the United States Naval Academy and a faculty associate in the graduate school at Johns Hopkins University. He is a coauthor of *Athena Rising: How and Why Men Should Mentor Women, The Elements of Mentoring,* and *Good Guys: How Men Can Be Better Allies for Women in the Workplace* (Harvard Business Review Press, 2020).

DEBORAH M. KOLB is the Deloitte Ellen Gabriel Professor for Women in Leadership (Emerita) and a cofounder of the Center for Gender in Organizations at Simmons College School of Management. An expert on negotiation and leadership, she is codirector of the Negotiations in the Workplace Project at the Program on Negotiation at Harvard Law School. She is a coauthor of *Negotiating at Work: Turn Small Wins into Big Gains* (Jossey-Bass, 2015).

MARYAM KOUCHAKI is an associate professor of management and organizations at Northwestern University's Kellogg School of Management. Her research focuses on decision making and ethics.

JENNIFER PETRIGLIERI is an associate professor of organizational behavior at INSEAD and the author of *Couples That Work: How Dual-Career Couples Can Thrive in Love and Work* (Harvard Business Review Press, 2019).

LAURA MORGAN ROBERTS is a professor of practice at the University of Virginia's Darden School of Business and the co-editor of *Race, Work and Leadership: New Perspectives on the Black Experience* (Harvard Business Review Press, 2019).

DAVID G. SMITH is a professor of sociology in the College of Leadership and Ethics at the United States Naval War College. He is a coauthor of *Athena Rising: How and Why Men Should Mentor Women* and *Good Guys: How Men Can Be Better Allies for Women in the Workplace* (Harvard Business Review Press, 2020).

ISAAC H. SMITH is an assistant professor of organizational behavior and human resources at BYU Marriott School of Business.

SCOTT SNOOK is an associate professor of organizational behavior at Harvard Business School. He served in the US Army Corps of Engineers for more than 22 years.

SCOTT TAYLOR is an associate professor of organizational behavior at Babson College.

ELLA F. WASHINGTON is a professor of practice at Georgetown University's McDonough School of Business and the founder of Ellavate Solutions, which provides executive coaching and diversity and inclusion strategy and training for organizations.

DEB ZEHNER has 15 years of experience conducting research, developing network-based assets, and leading organizational network projects, most recently with Connected Commons.

JOHN H. ZENGER is the CEO of Zenger Folkman, a leadership development consultancy. He is a coauthor of the book *Speed: How Leaders Accelerate Successful Execution* (McGraw Hill, 2016).

Index

Find fulfillment at home and at work with the HBR Working Parents Series